Most of us spend at least eight hours a day at work. Although you may not be able to choose or design the building you work in, you are probably in a position to make some minor changes that will make your workaday life more fulfilling.

Feng Shui for the Workplace is designed to show you how to make simple adjustments to your own work environment to become healthier, happier, and more successful in your career.

- Learn the most beneficial way to arrange your individual workspace, whether at home or at the office

- Discover eight interior feng shui remedies

- Improve the positive energy of your business' main entrance with a few minor adjustments

- Find out the most advantageous locations for your accounting department, sales department, boardroom, and lunchroom

- Discover the best areas for your company to seek new business

- Learn what to avoid when choosing a site for a new office

- Learn how to design business signage for growth and prosperity

About the Author

Richard Webster was born in New Zealand in 1946, where he still resides. He travels widely every year, lecturing and conducting workshops on psychic subjects around the world. He has written many books, mainly on psychic subjects, and also writes monthly magazine columns.

Richard is married with three children. His family is very supportive of his occupation, but his oldest son, after watching his father's career, has decided to become an accountant.

To Write to the Author

If you wish to contact the author or would like more information about this book, please write to the author in care of Llewellyn Worldwide, and we will forward your request. Both the author and publisher appreciate hearing from you. Llewellyn Worldwide cannot guarantee that every letter written to the author can be answered, but all will be forwarded. Please write to:

Richard Webster
℅ Llewellyn Worldwide
P.O. Box 64383, Dept. K808-7
St. Paul, MN 55164-0383, U.S.A.

Please enclose a self-addressed, stamped envelope for reply, or $1.00 to cover costs. If outside the U.S.A., enclose international postal reply coupon.

FENG SHUI

for

the

Workplace

RICHARD
WEBSTER

1998
Llewellyn Publications
St. Paul, Minnesota 55164-0383
U.S.A.

W

FIRST EDITION
First Printing, 1998

Cover design: Tom Grewe
Interior illustrations: Jeannie Ferguson
Book design: Amy Rost
Editing and typesetting: Marguerite Krause
Project management: Michael Maupin

Library of Congress Cataloging-in-Publication Data
Webster, Richard, 1946–
  Feng shui for the workplace / Richard Webster
  p. cm.
  Includes bibliographical references and index.
  ISBN 1-56718-808-7 (pbk.)
  1. Feng-shui. 2. Success in business. 3. Environmental
      psychology   I. Title.
  BF1779.F4W44   1998
  133.3'337—dc21   98-34579
                                     CIP

Llewellyn Publications
A Division of Llewellyn Worldwide, Ltd.
P.O. Box 64383, Dept. K808-7
St. Paul, Minnesota 55164-0383

Printed in the United States of America

Dedication

For Sunyar, Donna, Trish, Kim, and Carol

Acknowledgments

I would like to express my grateful thanks
to T'ai Lau for his help and advice.

Contents

Introduction

Feng shui is the ancient Chinese art of living in harmony with the environment. People in China and in neighboring cultures believe that if we harness the energies that are all around us, we will lead lives of happiness, contentment, and abundance. Most of us spend at least eight hours a day at work. It makes good sense to arrange our working environments so that we can harness these energies and be happy and successful in our chosen careers.

All over the East, business people regularly consult feng shui practitioners because they know that the proper use of feng shui gives them an extra edge in business. Citibank, Chase Asia, the Morgan Bank, Rothschild's, and even the *Wall Street Journal* are just a few examples of leading corporations that use feng shui.[1]

I know of many examples of people who have made changes to their work environment and become happier and more successful as a result. In my book *Feng Shui for Beginners*, I wrote of a friend of mine whose business was failing. As soon as he made a couple of changes based on the practice of feng shui, his business turned around and he is now an extremely wealthy and successful man.

Some years ago I was called in to evaluate the factory of a hosiery manufacturer. The company was having problems with high staff turnover, low morale, and a high incidence of illnesses. It was easy to see the cause of many of their problems. The ceiling of the factory was dark brown and felt like a depressing force weighing down all the staff. The company had expanded rapidly in the past and now had too much machinery in a confined area. This created problems when finished products had to be moved through the congested space.

The owners of the company moved the packaging area into the warehouse area, which made more space in the factory. They repainted the ceiling and the walls in pleasant, cheerful, light colors. They also allowed potted plants to be placed in certain areas to encourage the flow of ch'i, which is the universal life force in feng shui.

The results were amazing. Morale rapidly improved, production increased enormously, and staff members are no longer looking for other jobs because they are happy where they are.

An acquaintance of mine who had been a salesman for many years was promoted to sales manager at the printing ink manufacturing business for which he worked. He was thrilled with the promotion, but found himself unhappy in the new position. After looking at his office, I suggested that he change the position of his desk. He immediately found himself happier, more enthusiastic, and much more productive.

Virtually no work environment is perfect, but fortunately, most can be improved simply and easily by making a few minor adjustments. I have seen very few places that are total disasters.

This book is intended to show you how you can make any necessary changes in your own work environment, and become healthier, happier, and more successful in your career as a result.

1

What Is Feng Shui?

Feng shui is the art of living in harmony with the earth. Five thousand years ago, the people of China noticed that if they placed their homes to face the south, with hills behind them and gently flowing water in front, the people who lived in the home would lead happy, contented lives.

The words *feng shui* mean "wind and water." People noticed that the cold, harsh winter winds came from the north. The hills behind their homes protected them from the worst of these. Flowing water allowed the crops to grow and created ch'i energy.

Ch'i

Ch'i is the universal life force that is found in all living things. It is being created and dissipated all the time. When it is present, the earth smells sweet and everything goes exactly the way you want it. Ch'i is created whenever anything is done perfectly. A photographer who captures a glorious sunset is creating ch'i, as is a street cleaner who takes pride in his work and makes sure it is done perfectly.

Ch'i abounds where there is gently flowing water. Stagnant water creates negative ch'i, known as *shar ch'i*. If the water flows too quickly, all the ch'i is carried away. Consequently, it is better if the water slowly meanders on its way.

Visitors to Hong Kong frequently comment on the fact that every park contains a fountain. Some of these parks are tiny, but provide a welcome respite from the hustle and bustle that surrounds them. All of these fountains create beneficial ch'i.

We want to attract as much ch'i as possible into our home and work environments. When there is plenty of ch'i, we feel happy and contented.

Yin and Yang

Ch'i can be divided into two halves, known as *yin* and *yang*. It is believed that the first time ch'i moved it created yang (the male principle). When it rested, yin (the female principle) was created. Yin and yang together create a whole, and neither can exist on its own. The ancient Chinese never tried to define yin and yang. Instead, they delighted in coming up with lists of opposites, such as black and white, front and back, tall and short, male and female, shady and sunny. In fact, yin and yang first came about when the ancients noticed that the northern slopes of a mountain

Figure 1A: The yin/yang symbol

were shaded (yin), while the southern slopes were sunny (yang). The yin/yang symbol is a circle consisting of two tadpole-like shapes, one black with a white spot at one end (yin), the other white with a black spot (yang). The spot is another example of the belief that yin and yang should be in balance; wherever you find yin you will also find yang, and vice versa (Figure 1A).

The Dragon and the Tiger

Feng shui is an intriguing mixture of fact, myth, legend, and superstition. It is somewhere between an art and a science. The stories and beliefs that surround the subject are charming, but caused considerable frustration to Westerners when they were trying to colonize Hong Kong. This is because in feng shui, a green dragon or white tiger lives under every mountain. When the English wanted to make railway tunnels, they could not find any Chinese workers to help, because none of them were prepared to risk hurting these animals. Consequently, the British had to bring in non-Chinese laborers to do this work.

In fact, there are four main symbolic animals in feng shui. In the east lies the green dragon. To the west lies the white tiger. Where these two animals symbolically couple is the ideal place for a house or other building to be sited. Behind this house, to the north, lies the black tortoise. In front of the house, to the south, lies the red phoenix (Figure 1B).

The dragon and tiger create a horseshoe effect, and the hills that make up the dragon are always slightly higher than those of the tiger. The perfect spot to build a home is nestled in the middle of the horseshoe. If you locate yourself too close to the mouth of the dragon, you risk being snapped at. Likewise, if you are too close to the dragon's tail, you will be in trouble if he flicks or swings it.

Today, few people have the luxury of being able to choose an idyllic site that exactly matches the guidelines set by feng shui. Most of us have to use neighboring buildings to act symbolically as the tiger and dragon when we decide

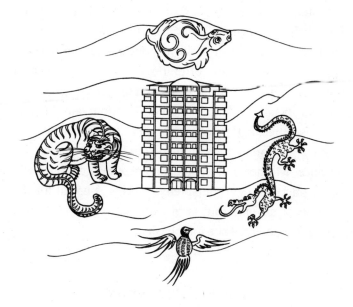

Figure 1B: The four symbolic animals

where we are going to live. We can also do this when choosing a suitable place for our business.

Theoretically, the perfect direction for our premises to face is south, with gentle hills (or other buildings) behind us to act as the tiger and dragon, and with gently flowing water in front of the building. (If you live in the Southern Hemisphere, the best direction to face is north. This is because the feng shui symbolism relating to the north and south compass positions are reversed. East and west remain the same for both hemispheres.)

Water symbolizes money to the Chinese. If the water flows behind our premises it means financial opportunities are lost. However, if it flows in front of our workplace it symbolizes financial opportunities that can be grasped. If there is no water in front of our premises, we can create some artificially, by building ponds or a fountain. Moving water is better than still water because the movement creates ch'i. A fountain in front of our main entrance, for instance, will not only create and encourage ch'i, but will also attract money to our premises. This is useful for the location of a home, but is of extreme importance when choosing a potential site for a business.

The Five Elements

The ancient Chinese believed that everything was composed of fire, earth, metal, water, or wood. These are the Five Elements of Chinese astrology. It would be more accurate to describe the elements as forces in which ch'i energy expresses itself in five different ways. If you were to have your Chinese horoscope drawn up, you would find that you are made up of most, or all, of these five symbolic elements. A number of people have asked me why air, one of the four elements of the ancient Greeks, was left out. In fact, the Chinese did consider it. Water vapor and clouds are considered to be part of the water element.

There is a Cycle of Production and a Cycle of Destruction for the five elements.

In the Cycle of Production, wood feeds fire, fire burns and leaves earth, in the earth we find metal, metal liquifies and produces water, and water nurtures and feeds wood (Figure 1C).

In the Cycle of Destruction, fire melts metal, metal destroys wood, wood draws from the earth, earth overpowers water, and water puts out fire (Figure 1D).

In the Appendix you can find out which element relates to your year of birth.

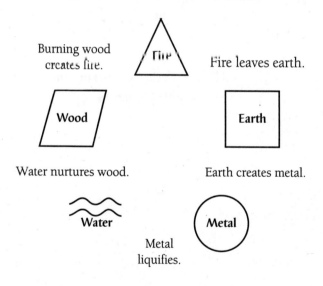

**Figure 1C: The Cycle of Production
of the Five Elements**

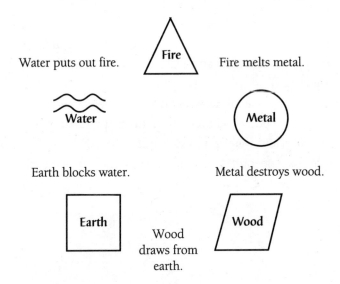

Water puts out fire.   Fire   Fire melts metal.

Water

Metal

Earth blocks water.   Metal destroys wood.

Earth

Wood
draws from
earth.

Wood

**Figure 1D: The Cycle of Destruction
of the Five Elements**

Fire

Direction: South
Color: Red
Planet: Mars

Fire is stimulating, exciting, and energetic. Fire people are active, busy people who always need something to look forward to. Fire's heat can warm, but it can also burn. Fire people are enthusiastic, outgoing, and unrestrained. When using their energies negatively, however, fire people become impulsive, overly outspoken and extravagant.

Earth

Direction: Center

Color: Brown, yellow, and orange

Planet: Saturn

Earth is stable, practical, honest, and conscientious. Earth people are loyal, attentive to detail, and loving. They work best in a harmonious environment. Negative earth people are obstinate and stubborn.

Metal

Direction: West

Color: White and metallic colors

Planet: Venus

Metal is competitive, enterprising, and business-minded. Metal people are shrewd, innovative, and astute. They are discriminating in their choices and appreciate having nice things around them. When using their abilities negatively, metal people are inclined to stretch the rules and be overly competitive.

Water

Direction: North

Color: Black and blue

Planet: Mercury

Water is intelligent, communicative, and adventurous. Water people enjoy learning and need intellectual challenges. The negative side of water people is that they tend to look down on people who are less intelligent than themselves.

Wood

Direction: East

Color: Green

Planet: Jupiter

Wood is creative, nurturing, and inspirational. Wood people enjoy new ideas and trying out new things. When using their abilities negatively, wood people become overly imaginative and seek to shock.

Shan

Mountains have always been important in feng shui. They provide protection from the harsh winds, of course, but they are also believed to be the home of dragons and gods. Mountains and hills are said to be yang. Flat land is described as yin. The ancient Chinese used the five elements to help them categorize the different types of hills and mountains they saw around them. *Shan* is the term used to describe their different shapes.

A conical mountain that rises to a sharp-pointed peak belongs to the fire element. This is because sharp points reminded the ancient Chinese of flames. It is a good location for people born under the earth element, but bad for someone belonging to metal.

A squared-top mountain, with a large flat summit, relates to the earth element. This is because the flat top reminded people that ground is often flat. This is a good location for people born under the metal element, but people born under the water element should avoid it.

Oblong mountains that are gently rounded belong to the metal element. This is because the rounded shape reminded the ancient Chinese of round coins. They are an excellent location for people born in water years, but are a negative site for people born under the wood element.

A ridged mountain, with wavy, tooth-like indentations on the top relates to the water element. This is because the undulating form of this type of mountain reminded the ancients of waves. This is a good location for people born under the wood element, but bad for people born in a fire year.

Round mountains that are narrow and steep, but are rounded at the summit, belong to the wood element. This is because these mountains reminded the Chinese of trees,

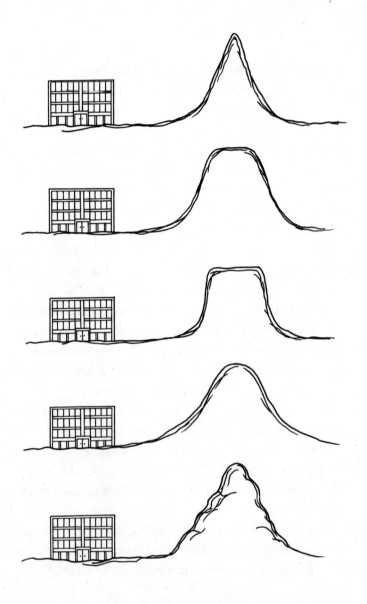

Figure 1E: Mountain shapes

which are usually straight and tall. They make a good location for people born in fire years, but should be avoided by people born in earth years (Figure 1E).

By using the elements, the ancients were able to determine if two adjacent mountains were compatible with each other. In Hong Kong there is an interesting example of incompatibility. The main peak of a mountain belongs to the wood element. However, at its feet stands Taip'ingshan, a small hill that belongs to the fire element. Ernest Eitel commented on this in his book *Feng Shui,* published in 1873. "Now, a pile of wood with fire at the bottom—what is the consequence?" he wrote. "Why, it is no wonder that most fires in Hong Kong occur in the Taip'ingshan district."[1]

Naturally, people compared the element of their birth with the elements of nearby hills and mountains to determine suitable places to live.

Today, it is common to use these mountain shapes to describe buildings.

> A triangular building belongs to the **fire** element.
>
> A square building relates to the **earth** element.
>
> A round building relates to the **metal** element.
>
> A ridged-top building relates to the **water** element.
>
> An oblong building relates to the **wood** element.

The Pa-kua

The origins of feng shui go back many thousands of years and are lost in the mists of time. There is a charming legend that says that feng shui began when a large tortoise crawled out of the Yellow River while irrigation work was in progress. The markings on the back of this tortoise formed a perfect magic square (Figure 1F). All the wise men of the day examined this auspicious happening, and ultimately came up with the beginnings of feng shui, the I Ching, Chinese numerology, and Chinese astrology.

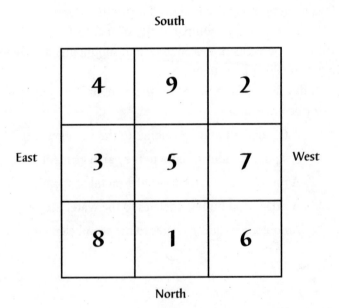

Figure IF: The magic square

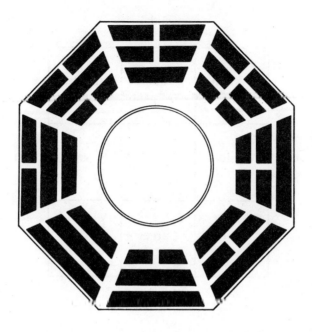

Figure 1G: The eight-sided pa-kua shape

This magic square also indicated the eight directions, all of which came to represent different aspects of a person's life. Ultimately, the magic square became an eight-sided figure known as the *pa-kua* (Figure 1G). Eight-sided figures are regarded as being especially favorable from a feng shui point of view. Recently I stayed in a hotel and noticed that every sign was pa-kua shaped. This was just one of many changes this hotel had made to improve its feng shui.

The eight aspects of a corporation's life, placed into a square shape for convenience, are shown in Figure 1H. The

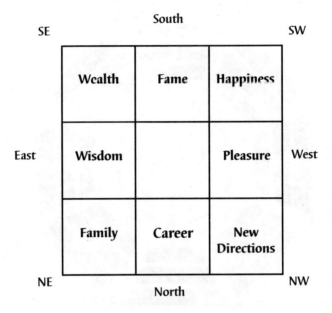

Figure 1H: The eight locations

eight directions are also shown for completeness. Traditionally, the south was the best direction for a building to face.

To use it with your own place of work, you need to find out the compass direction that the main entrance to the building is facing. The pa-kua is placed over a plan of your business premises, and can then be interpreted. Each area has a specific meaning.

Wealth

The Wealth location is situated in the southeast. It relates to money and the accumulation of wealth. It is a good position for the accounting department of a corporation, or for the office of the president.

Fame

The Fame location is in the south. It relates to the reputation and standing of the corporation. Consequently, this is a good site for the public relations department. It is also a good location for the sales department, because what the sales representatives do has a direct bearing on the reputation of the business.

Happiness

The Happiness location is in the southwest. It relates to happiness and contentment. It is a good position for the chairman of the board, or anyone else who is not directly involved in the day-to-day running of the business.

Wisdom

The Wisdom location is in the east. This area relates to wisdom, experience, and knowledge. It is a good location for the office of a senior member of the company who has had a great deal of experience in the business.

Pleasure

The Pleasure location is in the west. It relates to fun, laughter, and happiness. It is the ideal location for a lunch room, company gymnasium, or anything else relating to recreation and pleasure.

Family

The Family location is situated in the northeast. It relates to the well-being of the staff. This would be a good site for the employment office or the human resources department.

Career

The Career location is situated in the north. It relates to business planning and development. It is a good position for the boardroom.

New Directions

The New Directions location is in the northwest. It relates to new starts and improvements. It is a good location for the planning department, and anything else involved in the commencement of new projects.

Good Luck

The center of the pa-kua is the good luck area. It is sometimes referred to as the spiritual or soul center. This area needs to be kept well lit to encourage ch'i energy, which then spreads to every corner of the building.

It can be an interesting exercise to place the pa-kua over a plan of your premises in this way. You may find, for instance, that your sales department is in the Pleasure location. Imagine what that would do to sales! You may find that the bathrooms are in the Fame or Career locations.

Naturally, it is best to move the department to a more suitable area, but there are remedies that can be used when that is not possible.

Aspirations of the Pa-kua

What we have done so far with the pa-kua is use compass directions. This is not surprising, because the pa-kua plays a major role in the Compass School of feng shui.

However, there is another branch of the Compass School, known as the Aspirations of the pa-kua, that does not use the directions of the compass. Not surprisingly, the Aspirations are controversial, and many feng shui practitioners choose not to use them. I was shown how to use the Aspirations in Hong Kong many years ago. It is an extremely popular method of evaluation there, and has the advantage of convenience. You can instantly do an evaluation of any building without needing a compass or having to know any of the directions.

Wealth	Fame	Marriage
Family		Children
Knowledge	Career	Mentors

The main entrance is always on this side of the square

Figure 1J: The Aspirations of the Pa-kua

As in the previous method, the Aspirations of the Pa-kua uses a three-by-three magic square. However, some of the locations have different meanings (Figure 1J). It is usually used for homes, rather than businesses. However, it is commonly used for assessing individual offices and other rooms inside a business.

The pa-kua is placed over a plan of the building in such a way that the side of the pa-kua that contains Knowledge, Career, and Mentors is aligned with the wall of the building that contains the main entrance. Consequently, it makes no difference which direction the main entrance is facing. This means, for example, that the Wealth location is always as far diagonally to the left of the main entrance as possible.

The Mentors area is always as far to the right from the main entrance as possible.

When the Aspirations of the Pa-kua are used to evaluate an office, the side containing Knowledge, Career, and Mentors is aligned with the wall containing the main entrance to the room. The Aspirations can also be used to evaluate something as small as a desk. In this case, the side containing Knowledge, Career, and Mentors is aligned with the side of the desk where the person sits.

Wealth

This relates to money and finance. This is a good location for the office of the accountant or president. In the East, you will find a small metal dish containing coins in the Wealth position on many desks to help activate this area of the person's life.

Fame

This relates to the reputation and standing of the business in the community.

Marriage

In a home, this is the best location for the master bedroom. However, because it also applies to relationships in general, it can relate to harmonious dealings with members of the staff. This area can be activated with a feng shui remedy if you are having problems with morale or high staff turnover.

Family and Health

This area relates to family in a wide sense of the word. It means the people you love and care about. It is a good place to store the first aid kit.

Children

This area relates to young people. It can be used as the location of the employment office or for any other purpose that involves dealing with young people. At one time I worked for a large corporation that sent out regular mailings to schools. The Children area is the ideal location for any work of this nature.

Knowledge

This area relates to learning. In a home it is the ideal place to study or to keep books. In a business it is a good place for a staff training room.

Career

This area relates to progressing in one's chosen career. If the main entrance is in the middle of the front wall, the Career area is the first to be seen. It should be well lit and appear welcoming and friendly.

Mentors

Mentors are people who can offer advice. This area would make a good location for a conference room where the advice of such people can be sought.

Good Luck

The center area is known as the Good Luck center. In a home it is a good place to hang a chandelier, because that attracts beneficial ch'i, which can then be sent off around the house. This area also needs to be stimulated in the workplace. The best way of doing this is to increase the amount of light in this part of the building.

The Aspirations of the Pa-kua are not confined within the walls of the building, but spread out indefinitely. Consequently, the best place for the corporation to seek extra business (money) would be by prospecting in the direction indicated by the Wealth location. If the main entrance faced south, for instance, the wealth direction would be in the northwest.

Figure 1K shows the floor plan of a corporation that wholesales sporting equipment. We will look at it using both of the methods we have examined.

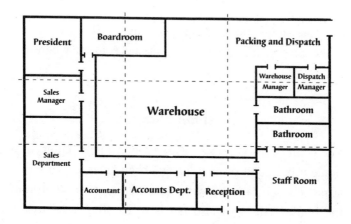

President	Boardroom		Packing and Dispatch
Sales Manager	Warehouse		Warehouse Manager / Dispatch Manager / Bathroom / Bathroom
Sales Department			
	Accountant / Accounts Dept. / Reception		Staff Room

Figure 1K: Evaluating a warehouse

Evaluation Using the Pa-kua and Compass Directions

The main entrance faces north. This means that the president's office and half of the boardroom are located in the Wealth location. Incidentally, in feng shui the best placement of the CEO's office is diagonally as far away from the main entrance as possible. This is the perfect location, and the president of this company will be able to concentrate on making the corporation as financially successful as possible.

The Fame location includes half of the boardroom and part of the warehouse. The placement of the boardroom is good, with half of it in the Wealth location and the remainder in the Fame area. Meetings in this room are likely to be highly productive. It would be a good idea to store the most prestigious brands of merchandise in this part of the warehouse to help the corporation's reputation.

The Happiness location consists mainly of the Packing and Dispatch departments, plus a small part of the warehouse. This area is likely to be a cheerful, happy place. The staff will cooperate and work well together. The people who deliver and pick up goods from this area will gain a good impression of the business.

The Wisdom location includes the sales manager's office, a third of the sales department, and a small part of the warehouse. From this position, the sales manager would offer good, sound advice, and is likely to be regularly called upon for his or her expertise in areas other than sales. The more senior sales staff should occupy the part of the sales department taken up by the Wisdom location.

The Pleasure location includes the offices of the warehouse and dispatch managers as well as the two bathrooms. The warehouse and dispatch managers would be likely to spend too much time in their offices and too little time dealing with their staff. They would be happy and contented with their jobs, but would need constant motivation to leave their offices and become involved in the warehouse and dispatch areas.

This is not a good place for the bathrooms, either, because the staff would be inclined to spend too much time there.

The Family location includes two-thirds of the sales department as well as the accountant's office. This is a good location for the sales department. The sales staff would be likely to treat all their customers as members of the family, creating close bonds with them. Each salesperson would also get along well with the rest of the sales staff. It is an unusual location for the accountant's office. This accountant would be more concerned with people than with figures. Staff members would come to him or her for help and advice.

The Career location includes most of the accounts department and half of the reception area. The accounts department would be motivated to achieve results. They are also likely to come up with good ideas concerning the growth of the corporation. This business should have a suggestions box hung up somewhere, to encourage staff members to write down their ideas.

Half of the reception area is taken up by the Career location as well. Any awards or trophies that the corporation has been awarded should be displayed here, as well as any favorable publicity.

The New Directions location consists mainly of the staff room, but includes half of the reception area as well. The staff are likely to come up with good ideas while spending time in the staff room. Senior management would benefit by listening to what the staff have to say in the relaxed atmosphere of this room.

It may seem that the reception area is wasted in this location. However, a good receptionist would receive valuable ideas and suggestions from visitors and should be encouraged to write these down and pass them on.

The Good Luck area is in the center of the warehouse. This is probably the best possible use of this area, because the corporation is, after all, a wholesaling business.

Evaluation Using the Aspirations of the Pa-kua

Interestingly enough, the president's office is also located in the Wealth location when we analyze the floor plan using the Aspirations of the Pa-kua. This is the perfect location, and the president is likely to be enthusiastic and motivated. Half of the boardroom is also included, and the excitement and enthusiasm will be evident there as well.

The Fame area includes half of the boardroom and part of the warehouse. This is good as far as the reputation of the company is concerned.

The Marriage area contains the packing and dispatch departments as well as part of the warehouse. People working here are likely to make friends with each other easily. They are also likely to spend time matchmaking for other members of the staff.

The Family area contains the sales manager's office and a third of the sales department. The sales manager is likely to be concerned about the well-being of his sales staff, and will strongly support them, even when sales volumes are down.

The Children area contains the bathrooms and the offices of the warehouse and dispatch managers. The two managers would find their offices comfortable places in which to conduct interviews. They would also find it particularly easy to deal with younger members of their staff here. However, younger members of the staff may not stay long as the bathrooms are also in this area. Water represents wealth in feng shui. In the bathrooms, wealth is flushed down the toilet. Consequently, in this location, wealth, meaning young talent, would symbolically be flushed away.

The Knowledge area includes two-thirds of the sales department and the accountant's office. The sales staff will be well versed and knowledgeable about the products they sell. This means they will approach their customers with confidence and be successful at their jobs. The accountant will also be skilled and knowledgeable in his field. He or she will be able to give valuable advice to the board members on all financial matters relating to the corporation.

The Career area includes half of the reception and most of the accounts department. The staff here will be motivated to progress in their careers. This could create problems with a medium-sized company which may not have sufficient openings to satisfy the personal ambitions of their staff.

The Mentors area contains the staff room and half of the reception area. People who have retired from this corporation are likely to return every now and then at lunchtime to talk about old times and give suggestions to current staff members. This area is likely to attract an older person to greet visitors to the business. This person would enjoy helping and offering advice to everyone who came in.

Naturally, the first of these evaluations will be changed if the building was somehow moved. If the building could be moved so that the main entrance faced west, the wealth area would then be located in the packing and dispatch departments. However, using the Aspirations of the Pa-kua, the Wealth location would always be in the president's office no matter which direction the main entrance faced.

It can be an interesting exercise to look at Figure 1H and mentally place the main entrance at each of the eight directions and see what differences you find. You will notice that some directions are much more favorable than others.

2

The Building

Most people are not able to choose or design their own building to work in. However, you are probably in a position to make some changes to your work environment that will make your working life more pleasant and enjoyable.

An acquaintance of mine is a quantity surveyor for a large construction company. He was finding his work extremely stressful and suffered from continual headaches. After evaluating his office, I was able to make some suggestions that made his work less stressful. I also indicated a nearby office, which was exactly the same size, where he would be much happier and, incidentally, more successful. The person occupying that office was also unhappy and was eager to swap. Since doing that, both of them are finding life easier and are coping with the constant demands upon them with little stress.

Not long ago, I met a man at a talk I gave who had recently returned from a two-year assignment in Europe. He had been very happy there and had not wanted to come back home. He said that being back in the head office was oppressive and made him feel ill. Outside his company's premises in Vienna was a large fountain in the middle of a small park. He had no idea that fountains had anything to do with feng shui but persuaded his employer to install one outside his company's head office. He immediately felt more comfortable working there. Incidentally, the corporation is also doing much better financially.

The three golden rules of real estate are: location, location, location. The location of your business is of vital importance to your success. Furthermore, this location varies depending on the type of business involved.

Most retailers, for instance, need to locate their stores where many people pass by. They also want to be visible from the road and have plenty of parking space available. A busy intersection may be the perfect place for them to set up business. This may not be as important to a specialist retailer with customers who are prepared to travel long distances to seek out him or her. I know an extremely good tailor in Long Beach, California, who is located in a small store in a side street. However, his customers travel hundreds of miles to see him because of the quality of his workmanship. Because of his skills and expertise, people are prepared to travel a long way to buy from him. Consequently, he could locate himself almost anywhere.

Someone working in an office will also want easy access and convenient parking, but may not need to be in the busiest and noisiest part of town. A quieter location in a side street may be perfect.

A factory should be located in an industrial area, and have room to expand. In this location there will be fewer problems with noise, waste, and traffic. It is also easier for large trucks to make pickups and deliveries.

You are fortunate if you are able to choose a site to build on. Look at the buildings and landscape around any proposed sites. Seek out the symbolic dragon and tiger. They will usually be created from nearby buildings. If there is flowing water nearby, make sure that the front door is facing it. If the water flows behind your building, it is a sign that you will become aware of financial opportunities but be unable to take advantage of them. Ideally, the water should be slow-moving or meandering. Your architect should design your building so that you can see as much of the water as possible.

It is also possible to place a pond or fountain in front of your business premises. This creates ch'i and attracts wealth. Century City in Los Angeles is a striking example of this. The fountains in the Avenue of the Stars have played a major role in attracting ch'i and wealth to this area.

It is also important that the back of your building be facing any hills. When the back of your building faces hills or other buildings, you are able to gain support from them. However, if the front faces them you will be deprived of any good luck and your venture is likely to stagnate and not move ahead.

You always want your back to be protected by the symbolic dragon and tiger. An acquaintance of mine who is an accountant was offered free rent for three months as an incentive to rent the thirty-fourth floor of a high-rise building. It was a prestigious site and he jumped at the opportunity. His offices had glorious views over the city in every

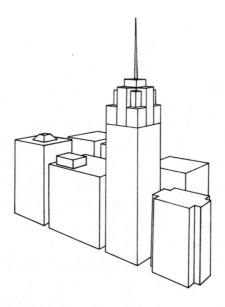

Figure 2A: An unprotected building

direction. Unfortunately, though, this meant that his back was no longer protected (Figure 2A). His business suffered and he was forced to sell his home to buy his way out of the lease. He is now working on the eighth floor of a less prestigious building and his business is booming. His back is protected by taller buildings and his offices have a glimpse of the harbor from the front. At first he found it hard to understand how his business could possibly be more successful operating from a location that was considerably lower in status than the high-rise building.

"I was just waiting to be knocked off," he told me. "I was like a tall poppy about to be mown down. Also, my clients feel that I'm giving them better value for money in my new premises." In fact, his charges are exactly the same, but his new premises give the impression of value for money.

Your building should harmonize and be in balance with the buildings that are already there. It is bad feng shui to work in a building that is much larger or smaller than its neighbors (Figure 2B). You can see examples of this in the industrial areas of any large city.

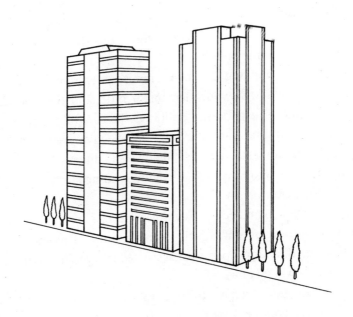

Figure 2B: Buildings not in harmony

Harmony also applies to road frontages. An acquaintance of mine ran two businesses from a single store. He thought it would be a good idea to turn his shop front into two distinct stores, one for each venture. However, it turned out to be disastrous and his turnover dropped alarmingly. His business recovered only when he turned the two stores back into one again. The reason for this was that his single storefront was approximately the same size as all the others in the block, which meant that they all harmonized. When he effectively halved the size of his shop, even though he had two of them, symbolically his neighbors benefited and he lost.

Make sure that the neighborhood is well balanced, with parks or other open spaces where the ch'i can accumulate. Areas of greenery provide yin energy which balances the yang energy of the buildings.

If you are building your own premises, design it so that it harmonizes with your element of birth and does not send shars to neighboring buildings. Be careful of sharp corners, roof lines, and mirrored or reflective glass. Your neighbors can retaliate and send any shars directly back to you. It is better to avoid accidentally sending shars out in the first place.

Mirrored, or reflective, windows are bad in feng shui because they prevent the ch'i from entering. This means that wealth and prosperity are restricted and profits for the business will go down.

Buildings that appear to have walls that are all glass are also not good, because the occupants are overly exposed and money trickles away. Make sure that large windows have curtains or blinds to control the amount of money you are prepared to lose.

It may be convenient to have parking under your building, but it is bad from a feng shui point of view. This is particularly so if the parking garage is open to the public. The activity from all the cars gradually weakens the businesses that are operating over the garage.

Buildings with a regular shape are much better from a feng shui perspective than those with unusual shapes. Square, oblong, round, and pa-kua (eight-sided) shapes are all good from a feng shui perspective. Buildings in the shape of a cross or triangle are considered bad. Harmony is the aim, of course, and your building can be any shape at all as long as it is aesthetically pleasing and does not send harmful shars to your neighbors.

Buildings conform to the five elements in exactly the same way that mountains do. Ideally, the building you work in harmonizes with your own personal element. Fortunately, there are things that you can do if you have to work in a building that does not relate well with your personal element.

Fire

Shape: Triangular

Fire element buildings contain sharp angles and pointed roofs or spires. The pyramid at the Louvre in Paris is a perfect example of a fire element building and harmonizes beautifully with the more traditional water element shape of the Louvre itself. This is not a good building for people of the metal element to work in, but it is excellent for people belonging to earth. If you belong to the metal element and have to work in a fire element building, you need something that represents the earth element to act as a cure. A small pottery or porcelain object will serve this purpose, as will anything that is yellow or orange.

Earth

Shape: Square

Earth element buildings are low and flat, with flat-topped roofs. Many office buildings and apartment blocks belong to the earth element. Some houses belong to both the earth and fire elements, because the house is square, but the roof slopes. Earth buildings are excellent for storage purposes. Earth buildings are not good for people born under the water element, but are ideal for people of the metal element. If you belong to the water element and have to work in an earth building, you need to have something in your workspace that belongs to the metal element. Anything made of metal, preferably silver or gold, or an object white in color will act as a remedy.

Metal

Shape: Circular, round

Buildings that have domes, curved roofs, and arches are described as belonging to the metal element. Metal buildings are usually constructed for some religious or civic purpose. Metal relates strongly to money, so it is not surprising that many banks have domed ceilings. The famous Guggenheim Museum in New York is an excellent example of a metal element building, with its graceful curves and circular appearance. Metal element buildings are not good for people of the wood element, but are excellent for water people. If you belong to the wood element and have to work in a metal element building, you need something that relates to the water element in your work area. An aquarium, small fountain, or anything that is blue or black will provide effective remedies.

Water

Shape: Square, flat

Water fits into any shape, and water element buildings undulate and often appear to be a mixture of the other four elements. The Houses of Parliament in London are a good example of the water element. Water element buildings are not good for fire element people, but are excellent for people of the wood element. If you belong to the fire element and have to work in a water element building, anything made of living wood or green in color will serve as an effective remedy. Potted plants and fresh flowers are good examples of objects to place in your work area.

Wood

Shape: Columnar, rectangular

Wood element buildings are tall and rectangular. They usually have flat roofs. Most skyscrapers belong to the wood element. Memorial columns, watchtowers, obelisks, and other tall, thin structures belong to the wood element. The Washington Monument is an excellent example of a wood element building. Wood element buildings are not good for earth element people, but are ideal for people born under the fire element. If you belong to the earth element and have to work in a wood element building, anything that belongs to the fire element makes a good remedy. A small, attractive object that is red in color is ideal.

Once you have determined the type of building you work in, you can evaluate it further. Place a pa-kua over the floor plan and ensure that all the important functions of your particular business are in the most suitable places. For instance, you would not want the bathrooms to be in the Wealth location, or your sales people to be in the Pleasure location. These are extremes, of course, but if you are erecting your own building, you will be able to make good use of feng shui during the planning stages.

Most of us are not in a position to design and construct our own premises and have to find an existing building to work in. All of the same criteria apply. As well as looking at the building you are planning to lease, examine the neighboring buildings to see what effect, if any, they have on the

Figure 2C: Building at a T-junction

one you are considering. There is a remedy for most things. However, if the mirrored surface of a neighboring building sends a strong glare toward your premises, it is probably better to find another site, because it is extremely difficult to eliminate that particular shar.

If you are considering leasing a store, ensure that all the stores in the block have approximately the same amount of road frontage.

Avoid locating your business at a T-junction (Figure 2C). You may feel that the business will benefit by the increased exposure it receives from all the passing traffic, but in reality, a shar is a disaster waiting to happen. It might take time, but eventually it will damage your business. This location is particularly bad if the shar heads directly toward your main entrance.

A short while ago I was employed as a consultant to feng shui a large shopping mall. It was an extremely successful mall, but several of the stores were never successful and the mall managers wanted to know why. Three of the sites were at the end of long passages, each of which created a shar. The others had entrances directly facing escalators that headed downward toward them. In all of these situations, you would expect the stores to gain business because so many people headed directly toward them. However, as long as the situation lasted no business was able to survive there.

The mall wanted to lease these empty stores and changed the placement of their entrances so they were no longer directly facing a shar. The last time I visited the mall, all of the empty stores had been leased and the occupants appeared to be thriving.

Many businesses are located in commercial buildings with land around them. The grounds should always be landscaped to help create a proper balance of yin and yang energy. This area also provides an attractive place for staff and visitors to sit or walk in during their breaks. A pond or fountain in front of the building is good feng shui. It provides good ch'i and helps create wealth. An artificial stream signifies abundance and can be very useful. Make sure that it meanders and does not travel in a straight line. As you know, straight lines create shars, so make sure that any paths or walkways also curve or meander.

Numbers, Names, and Signs

The number of your business address is also important. Each number has a meaning that can be interpreted. Interestingly enough, these meanings bear little relationship to traditional numerology, even though both disciplines are derived from the tortoise that crawled out of the Yellow River thousands of years ago.

The Chinese enjoy homonyms, which are words that sound alike but have different meanings. For instance, the Cantonese words for "four" and "death" sound the same. Consequently, Chinese people avoid the number four in their homes and businesses because it reminds them of death. "Two" sounds like the word for "easy." Therefore, if your business premises are at number 24, the address sounds like "easy death." The word "eight" sounds like "prosperity," which agrees perfectly with the numerological interpretation of eight, which is "money in the near future." This means that number 28 is a good address, because it means "easy money."

In feng shui the numbers are interpreted individually. In numerology, the numbers are usually added up and then reduced down to a single digit. This means that number 174 would be interpreted as a 3 in numerology, because 1 + 7 + 4 = 12, and 1 + 2 = 3. However, in feng shui we interpret each number individually. Incidentally, 174 is not a good combination in feng shui because it sounds like "everyone dying together."

Number One relates to the water element. It has no specific meaning, but is considered a highly positive number.

Number Two relates to the earth element. It is one of the two unlucky numbers and is related to ill health.

Number Three relates to the wood element. It is related to conflict, stress, anger, and disagreements.

Number Four relates to the wood element. It relates to love, sex, and knowledge.

Number Five relates to the earth element. It is the other unlucky number and is related to misfortune and oppression.

Number Six relates to the metal element. It is a highly positive number that relates to conservation of money.

Number Seven relates to the metal element. It signifies prosperity, and is also related to communication and spirituality.

Number Eight relates to the earth element. It is considered to be the most positive number and relates to prosperity in the near future.

Number Nine relates to the fire element. It is a positive number that represents good luck and future success.

All of this is complicated further, because the Chinese use traditional numerological interpretations as well as the feng shui ones. In fact, many Chinese people are not familiar with the feng shui meanings and are surprised to find that number two, for instance, is a negative number, because they interpret it as meaning "easy."

The feng shui numbers are also used to create auspicious personalized number plates for business vehicles. Even the final digits of telephone numbers and credit cards are carefully examined in the East to ensure that they are favorable. Banks and telephone companies are used to people asking for these numbers to be changed to digits that the owners think will be more successful.

The name of the corporation is also carefully evaluated in the East. Traditionally, the number of strokes in each character of the name of the corporation was totalled and interpreted. A character formed from an even number of brush strokes was classified as yin, while an odd number of brush strokes was yang. The aim was to have approximately an equal number of yin and yang elements in the name. The first character in every word forming the name of the corporation was related to one of the five elements. Naturally, there had to be a balance between the elements, and names were devised using the Productive Cycle of Elements.

Great emphasis is also placed on the signs hung up to advertise the business. Yin and yang are taken into account when determining the size of a sign. If one side consists of an odd number of inches, the other side has to be even, to create a balance of yin and yang.

Naturally, the sign has to be pleasant to look at, and should not create any shars. It should be neither too large nor too small in relation to the size of the building to which it is attached. It should not block or cast shade on any windows or doors. The best shapes are square, oblong, pa-kua (eight-sided), or round. Triangular shapes are not desirable because the triangle symbolizes the fire element, which is potentially dangerous. This is particularly the case if the triangle points downward. The message on the sign should be clear and easy to understand. In other words, the sign should be pleasant to look at and draw attention to the business.

Brightly colored neon signs are good because the light attracts ch'i. You cannot spend more than five minutes in Las Vegas or in the Ginza area of Tokyo without realizing the incredible power of neon lighting. In the evenings these bright lights signify and promote activity.

The colors used on the sign should include the color that relates to the business owner's personal element. Any other colors should harmonize with this color using the Productive Cycle of Elements. Traditionally, an odd number of colors was always used. Signs containing either three or five colors are said to be ideal because they signify business growth and prosperity. A sign containing an even number of colors is not as auspicious or as effective in attracting customers.

The most successful combinations of colors contain the following elements:

> Water, Wood, Fire (Blue or Black, Green, and Red)
>
> Wood, Fire, Earth (Green, Red and Yellow, or Brown)
>
> Fire, Earth, Metal (Red, Yellow, or Brown, and White, Silver, or Gold)

Earth, Metal, Water (Yellow or Brown, White, Silver, or Gold, and Blue or Black)

Metal, Water, Wood (White, Silver, or Gold, Blue or Black, and Green)

The choice of colors is not quite as important if the building is owned by an absentee landlord. However, many people believe that the personal element of the owner of the business should still be represented. Here are the colors that relate to the eight directions that the sign could face:

North: Yellow, white, and red, or white, red, and green.

Northeast: Yellow, white, and red, or white, red, and green, or red.

East: Blue or black, green and red, or green, red, and white or gold.

Southeast: White or gold, red, and green.

South: White or gold, green, and yellow, or white or gold, yellow, and red.

Southwest: White or gold, red and yellow, or white or gold, green, and red.

West: White or gold, blue or black, and yellow, or yellow, white or gold and red.

Northwest: Red, yellow and white or gold.

Some colors have become strongly associated with certain types of businesses. Gold and red are most frequently associated with Chinese restaurants, for instance. This is because red signifies good luck and gold signifies money. However, red also relates to the fire element, and fire, or heat, is required to cook the food. Many jewelry stores use white, because this color relates to the metal element.

Many signs include the corporation's logo or emblem. These should be used with care. It is better to leave the logo off the sign if the design includes triangles, crosses, or arrows that point downward.

3

The Main Entrance

The first thing people see when they come to visit you at your place of work is the actual building and any grounds that might surround it. Hopefully, these create a positive impression. If you have gardens outside, make sure that they are well tended and look attractive. Trees, shrubs, and flowers all create ch'i which can benefit your business. Trees can also provide protection from shars coming from neighboring businesses. A fountain or pond outside the front of the business will also create ch'i and stimulate prosperity and success.

The path leading to your main entrance should be kept tidy, and the entrance itself should look inviting. Ideally, the path leading to your entrance should curve or meander, because a straight path leading directly to the front door creates a shar.

Make sure that no shars are attacking your main entrance. Check the roof lines of neighboring buildings and any straight lines or sharp angles that might be directed at your front door. Look for any shars that may be inside your own property. A single tree directly in front of your front door may be a shar, for instance. This is certainly the case if any branches point directly toward your front door. Correct any shars that you are able to change or block. You might change a straight path into a gently curving one, for example. A mirror can be used to reflect other shars back where they came from. Remember, if you cannot see a shar it ceases to exist. A hedge or screen may be all that is required to eliminate the problems caused by a shar.

You may decide to place stone or metal lions or other animals beside your main entrance to symbolically protect the building. The Hongkong and Shanghai Bank in Hong Kong has two large, bronze lions, Stephen and Stitt, who guard the main entrance to the bank. When the bank's new building was opened, cranes were used to put the two lions in position simultaneously to prevent either lion from becoming jealous of the other.[1]

The door should be in keeping with the size of the building. Your main entrance is the most important place for ch'i to enter your premises. An entrance that is too small will constrict the amount of ch'i that can come in. Conversely, an entrance that is too large will allow wealth to escape.

Many years ago, the Hang Seng Bank in Hong Kong was taken over by the Hongkong Bank. This bank, formerly the second largest in Hong Kong, had failed because the main entrance of the head office looked like a huge mouth that was unable to close. Consequently, all the money was able to escape.[2]

The main entrance should be well lit and easy to find. Sometimes it is hard to determine which entrance is the main one. If your visitors have problems determining which entrance to use, the ch'i will also experience similar difficulty.

You may have underground parking or a parking area that leads to a side entrance, rather than the main one. This is fine just as long as your visitors have no problems in finding the lobby once they are inside.

If possible, the front door should face in the direction most favorable for the person who owns the business. These directions are determined based on the person's year of birth.

Best Directions for Men Born in Each Year

North: 1918, 1927, 1936, 1945, 1954, 1963, 1972, 1981, 1990, 1999

Northeast: 1911, 1920, 1929, 1938, 1947, 1956, 1965, 1974, 1983, 1992

East: 1916, 1925, 1934, 1943, 1952, 1961, 1970, 1979, 1988, 1997

Southeast: 1915, 1924, 1933, 1942, 1951, 1960, 1969, 1978, 1987, 1996

South: 1910, 1919, 1928, 1937, 1946, 1955, 1964, 1973, 1982, 1991

Southwest: 1914, 1917, 1923, 1926, 1932, 1935, 1941, 1944, 1950, 1953, 1959, 1962, 1968, 1971, 1977, 1980, 1986, 1989, 1995, 1998

West: 1912, 1921, 1930, 1939, 1948, 1957, 1966, 1975, 1984, 1993

Northwest: 1913, 1922, 1931, 1940, 1949, 1958, 1967, 1976, 1985, 1994

Best Directions for Women Born in Each Year

North: 1914, 1923, 1932, 1941, 1950, 1959, 1968, 1977, 1986, 1995

Northeast: 1912, 1918, 1921, 1927, 1930, 1936, 1939, 1945, 1948, 1954, 1957, 1963, 1966, 1972, 1975, 1981, 1984, 1990, 1999

East: 1916, 1925, 1934, 1943, 1952, 1961, 1970, 1979, 1988, 1997

Southeast: 1917, 1926. 1935, 1944, 1953, 1962, 1971, 1980, 1989, 1998

South: 1913, 1922, 1931, 1940, 1949, 1958, 1967, 1976, 1985, 1994

Southwest: 1924, 1933, 1942, 1951, 1960, 1969, 1978, 1987, 1996

West: 1911, 1920, 1929, 1938, 1947, 1956, 1965, 1974, 1983, 1992

Northwest: 1919, 1928, 1937, 1946, 1955, 1964, 1973, 1982, 1991

Another way of choosing the correct placement for the main entrance to your business is to use the element of your year of birth.

> If your element is **fire,** the best direction for your main door is south.

> If your element is **earth,** the best directions for your main entrance are southwest and northeast.

> If your element is **metal,** the best directions for your main entrance are west and northwest.

> If your element is **water,** the best direction for your main entrance is north.

> If your element is **wood,** the best directions for your main entrance are east and southeast.

You can use this information to analyze the entrance of your current place of work and see if the ch'i of the building matches your personal ch'i. You will remember that there is a Cycle of Destruction (fire melts metal, metal chops wood, wood draws from earth, earth quenches water). There is also a debilitating cycle (fire destroys wood, wood drains water, water rusts metal, metal comes from earth, earth quenches fire).

Consequently, if your element is fire, west and northwest are bad directions for your main entrance to face (because they belong to the metal element). Likewise, east and southeast are also bad (because fire destroys wood).

However, southwest and northeast are both good directions for you, because earth follows fire in the Productive Cycle of Elements (fire produces earth, earth provides metal, metal liquifies like water, water nurtures wood, wood burns, creating fire).

Your career will progress more smoothly if you check out the main entrances of potential places of work before accepting the job.

To further complicate the issue, the ancient Chinese believed that it was best to orient the main entrance to either the south or southeast. This is because they felt that south indicated good luck flowing toward the business. Southeast was even more propitious, because they felt that it indicated wealth flowing toward the business. Consequently, it is best to experiment with these considerations and decide which direction feels best for you. It is important to remember that a main entrance that is free of shars is better than an entrance that faces a good direction but is threatened by shars.

In Hong Kong, it is common to see entrance doors set at an angle to the street to ensure that the entrance direction is favorable to the owner of the business.

Revolving doors are considered good in feng shui because they do not send shars on neighboring buildings.

The front doors should open inward to encourage the ch'i in. Naturally, any fire or other emergency doors should open outward to allow the ch'i out. I have seen many businesses that have two sets of front doors. One set opens outward to fit in with the city's regulations, while the second set opens inward to encourage the ch'i inside.

It is important that the back entrance not be in a direct line from the main entrance. When the doors are in line, all the ch'i that comes in the front entrance will immediately go out again through the back door. A suitable remedy for this problem is to put up a screen so that the back door cannot be seen from the main entrance.

The entrance lobby should be well lit and appear spacious. If it is small, a large mirror can symbolically make it appear twice its actual size. The lobby should also appear welcoming. All businesses need customers and the more welcoming the entrance area is, the more likely people are to enter the building.

A large lobby area is much better than a small one. The lobby gathers up positive ch'i before sending it around the building. A large lobby can collect much more ch'i than a small one. All this positive ch'i also prevents negative ch'i from coming in.

If the receptionist is stationed in the lobby area, he or she should not face the front door directly because this can prove intimidating to any visitors.

Escalators and elevators directly facing the main entrance are bad from a feng shui point of view because they confuse the ch'i. Much of the ch'i is lost or dissipated in this situation. It is better if the escalators and elevators are at an angle to the entrance.

Probably the most famous example of this is the head office of the Hongkong and Shanghai Bank, where the position of the escalators was altered to allow the "up" escalators to encourage more money into the bank. The "down" escalators were also moved to discourage money from leaving the business.

The lobby area gives your visitors a number of clues about you and your business. The color scheme, lighting, furnishings, temperature, and smell all give information to your prospective clients. We all gain information like this all the time, often without realizing that we are doing it. Would you experience different feelings walking into a dim, gloomy, musty lobby than you would going into a spacious, bright, and well-lit lobby? Of course you would.

Some years ago my dentist retired and I had to find a new one. A business associate recommended someone to me and I decided to pay a visit to this dentist. He had offices in an old building that should have been condemned. The lobby area was dimly lit and had a foul smell. I did not go upstairs to his office because I had already completely lost faith in someone who would run his practice from such dingy surroundings.

A few days later, I told the person who had recommended this dentist to me about my experience.

"You should have gone up," my associate said. "His offices are very pleasant."

That may have been the case, but the lobby was so unpleasant that I never went upstairs to find out more about the dentist. It would be interesting to know how many potential clients this dentist has lost over the years because of the condition of his main entrance.

Naturally, a store selling fruit and vegetables would use different methods of attracting customers inside than would an exclusive jewelry store. A firm of lawyers or accountants will try to give an impression of stability and success to people as they come in. A factory might try to convey the impression of activity and success. Image is of great importance, and you have the opportunity to make a good first impression only once. The dentist I intended to visit obviously did not realize that.

It may seem that retail establishments are the only businesses that need be overly concerned with the appearance of the main entrance. After all, what difference would a change in the entrance of a factory make? Most customers never get to visit the factory anyway. However, even if no customer ever visited, the look of the main entrance is still important. The front of the building is like a face and the door is the mouth. We want as much ch'i as possible to come into the mouth to benefit everyone who is working inside. We also want the working environment to be as pleasant as possible to ensure the happiness and good health of everyone working there. When the feng shui is good, all the workers will produce more and will also feel contented and happy.

Obviously, retail stores want to attract as many people inside as possible. Many other types of businesses limit the people who can enter. A wholesaler, for instance, may not allow the general public inside. Other businesses see people only by appointment.

It makes no difference what type of customer you want to attract. Your main entrance needs to be looked after to encourage both ch'i and your customers inside.

4

The Interior Layout

The interior layout of your business premises should allow all the essential functions of the business to flow as smoothly as possible. I find it helpful to imagine that I am the ch'i energy that wants to visit every part of the building. Occasionally, it is possible to do this almost effortlessly. Usually, though, there are problem areas that disrupt the movement of ch'i. Often this is due to poor traffic flow.

I remember visiting a factory where the passageways were just wide enough to allow a pallet-load of supplies through. This meant that everyone using the passage at the same time as a pallet-load of goods had to move out of the way to let the pallet pass. This was not efficient and caused a great deal of aggravation.

A printing company I did business with had their paper cutter in a separate shed across a courtyard from the main factory. Any paper that needed to be cut or trimmed would have to be hauled through the factory and across the courtyard to where the cutter operator worked. This was inconvenient and time-consuming. Frequently, the work would pile up and be left waiting in the courtyard. The extra space was useful in fine weather, but in wet weather the corporation had major problems, both in storage and in getting the paper to the cutter. The managers deliberated for several years before they shifted the cutting and packing areas. This brought the paper cutter closer to the printing presses, cutting down on labor and time. The workers in the packing department were also delighted to have their own separate area in the shed.

Stores

Once the customer has entered our place of business, we want him or her to stay and look at what we have to offer. Consequently, the interior needs to be well lit and maintained at a pleasant temperature. The customer will not stay if the interior is too hot or too cold. Our merchandise should be displayed as attractively as possible. It should be readily accessible. People will take their business elsewhere if they cannot examine the merchandise before buying. The sales staff should not face away from the main entrance.

Mirrors should be used to help create feelings of spaciousness, abundance, and prosperity. This is because they symbolically "double" the amount of everything they reflect. Now you know why you frequently see mirrors behind the drink bottles in bars. They symbolically double the amount of alcohol for sale.

Customers become upset and agitated if the store is crammed with shelves and displays and there is no room to move. There must be sufficient room for the customers to move around the store freely and easily.

The placement of the cash register is of vital importance. It should be placed at an angle to the front door. If it directly faces the front door, it will tend to intimidate potential customers. The person operating the cash register should have a good view of the exits to discourage shoplifting. The cash register should be free of any shars, because this will affect the success of the business. In Asia, it is common to place a mirror close to the cash register. This symbolically doubles the amount of money placed into the till.

Hanging a crystal or wind chime over the cash register causes the ch'i to rise, which encourages extra business.

The customer should be able to leave the store easily after completing his or her purchase.

Different types of stores have different requirements. A bookstore, for instance, has a different purpose and different needs than a beauty shop. In a bookstore, the various categories of books should be clearly marked to help the customers find what they are looking for. A bookstore also should not have direct sunlight shining into the premises; that could damage the books.

A beauty salon should look bright and appealing. The seats should be comfortable, and the shampooing and washing areas should provide sufficient privacy. There should be adequate ventilation to eliminate the different odors that are produced.

Sufficient aisle space is important in supermarkets. Our local supermarket has narrow aisles, which cause congestion and aggravation. Even worse, people walking past the loading bay on their way to the supermarket are exposed to a constant foul smell. There is not enough room behind the checkouts for people waiting to pay for their goods, and this also causes tempers to fray. Not surprisingly, my wife and I drive one mile farther to do our shopping at another supermarket which has none of these problems.

Factories

Too much noise is a problem in many factories. This creates negative ch'i. Incidentally, the same thing occurs when the business premises are too quiet. It is generally easier to add sound than take it away, but sound-proofing techniques are available. After I consulted with a metal-forming corporation, the owners placed large blocks of a foam material around the area where a huge die-stamping machine stamps out metal shapes all day long. The staff in this factory used to complain of headaches and were frequently absent. Once the noise levels were brought under control, these problems virtually disappeared.

Consideration needs to be given to the layout of the factory floor. The passageways need to be wide enough to satisfy all of the factory's needs. Avoid T-junctions where one passageway meets another. Do not place any machine or worker at the end of a passageway, because the straight line creates a shar that will affect his or her output. Many factories have overhead beams which also cause shars. Do not place any worker directly underneath these.

There should be sufficient light and ventilation in every factory. Large factories can often be cold places to work in. They are difficult to heat, of course, but a difference of a few degrees in temperature can have a huge effect on the volume and quality of the work produced.

We want as much ch'i as possible on the factory floor. Ch'i can be encouraged by sufficient light and cheerful colors. If the factory appears attractive, more ch'i will come into the building, and the morale and contentment of the workers will increase.

Warehouses

Most of the information about factories applies to warehouses as well. The important attributes for warehouses are sufficient space and adequate lighting. Frequently, as corporations grow, the warehouse stays the same size but has more and more stock stored in it. Eventually, stock is stored in the aisles and the staff members have problems maneuvering around it. Consequently, their jobs become harder to do and morale—and the amount of work accomplished—goes down.

Lighting is important in warehouses. Dim or poorly lit corners repel the ch'i and can bring financial problems to the business. Ideally, the lighting should be even and non-reflective. Curtains or blinds should be used wherever there is glare from the sun.

Areas that are damp or smelly create negative ch'i. They can also ultimately ruin the stock. Regular maintenance is required everywhere in your business premises. Doors that stick, windows that jam, and other minor niggling problems create negative ch'i and should be fixed as soon as the problem occurs.

Often, warehouses have two or more exits and drafts become a problem. Feng shui means "wind and water," but the feng shui ideal is gentle breezes, not drafts that send all the ch'i out of the warehouse. It is a good idea to have just one entrance open on days when the weather causes problems with heavy rain or wind.

Offices.

In the next chapter we will be discussing individual offices. Generally, the president's office should be the one farthest away from the main entrance. It also should be larger than the other offices to indicate this person's seniority and status.

The worst position for your office is at the end of a long hallway, because the corridor acts as a poison arrow heading directly to your entrance. Ultimately, this will affect your health and career. Just as bad are offices that directly face elevators and escalators, because it is believed that they will carry your wealth away.

It is much better to have an office on either side of a hallway. However, you do not want your entrance to face a bathroom on the opposite side of the hallway. This is considered a major shar, because the bathroom would send negative ch'i toward your office. The remedy for this is to keep your door shut as much as possible and to hang a mirror on it to reflect the bathroom back across the hallway.

If your office faces a doorway on the other side of the hallway, the two doors should be similar in size and be directly opposite each other. If the two doors are slightly offset, the occupants are likely to have disagreements (Figure 4A). The remedy is to place a mirror on the wall next to both doors.

Long, straight hallways create shars and send the ch'i racing through them. If there is a window at the end of the hallway, the ch'i will leave through it. This is why people working in this sort of environment often lack energy. The remedy is to slow down the ch'i energy. This can be done by placing mirrors at regular intervals along the hallway.

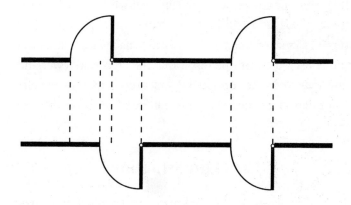

Figure 4A: Office door alignment

Alternatively, wind chimes or a hanging crystal can be used to attract and slow down the ch'i.

It is bad feng shui if your office door opens onto a staircase heading upward. This means that you have to come down the stairs every time you go to your office, which represents descending fortunes. It is much better to have your office door at the top of a flight of stairs, because this represents ascending fortunes. Also, as ch'i rises you will have more energy and vitality if your office is at the top of a flight of stairs.

It is also bad feng shui if your business occupies an entire floor of an office building, but does not have an enclosed reception area where people can be met when they come out of the elevator. This means that every time a visitor comes to your floor the feng shui of the area is disrupted. I used to do work for a company of event planners who occupied a floor in a high-rise building. Their entire floor was open-plan, which meant that whenever the elevator stopped at their floor everyone in the corporation turned to see who had arrived. It also made any visitors feel self-conscious, with the result that they received fewer and fewer visitors. The continual distractions caused by the elevator played a major role in the failure of the business.

The Eight Situations

In the East, certain directions are considered better for particular tasks than others. Traditionally, buildings faced south and the pa-kua was placed on top of the plan to decide the correct locations before construction began.

In time, buildings were constructed that faced in a variety of directions, but the traditional ideas of certain directions being better than others continued. For instance, in a building facing south, the Wealth location would be in the southeast. Many feng shui practitioners consider southeast to be the wealth location, no matter what direction the building faces. This theory is known as the Eight Situations and is part of the Compass School of feng shui.

Consequently, the southeast corner of the building is a good location for the accountant or CEO. The human resources manager or personnel department should be in the east (Family location). Research and development staff should be in the northeast (Knowledge sector). New staff should be in the north or west (Career and Children sectors). The advertising and promotional staff should be in the south (Fame sector). Staff training should be conducted in the northwest (Mentors area).

I bear this information in mind when doing a consultation, but I personally prefer to use the Aspirations of the Pa-kua, a method that determines locations based on the placement of the main door.

Recently, I did an evaluation for a firm of stockbrokers who were moving into new premises. Using the Aspirations of the Pa-kua would have placed the CEO's office in a position overlooking sewage ponds. This would have been disastrous from a feng shui point of view, because the negative ch'i coming from the ponds created a major shar. The only practical remedy would have been to keep the curtains pulled all the time. However, using the Eight Locations, it was possible to place the CEO's office in the southeast, a location with a pleasant view overlooking a large park and the tall buildings of downtown.

5

Office Layouts

Your office should be comfortable and reflect something of your personality. Make sure that the door to your room is protected from shars coming from outside your office. Anything that points toward or heads toward your door in a straight line is a poison arrow that needs to be remedied. You might be able to use something to hide the shar at its source. Potted plants can be good for this. If this is not possible, a small mirror on the outside of your door will send the shar back where it came from.

Usually it is good to have an outside view, but glaring light from the window can make it hard to work effectively. Blinds or drapes should be used to eliminate this problem during the appropriate times of day.

Ideally, your office should be square or oblong in shape. Sharp angles caused by L-shaped rooms or protruding corners are shars which need to be remedied. About a year ago, I visited a man who had four protruding corners in his office. He had used a different remedy for every corner and

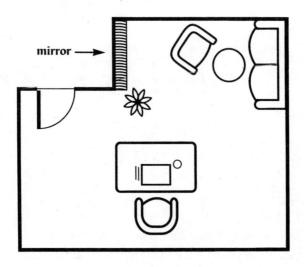

mirror ➔

Figure 5A: Feng shui remedy for office shar

wanted me to see the result. The remedies had been done discreetly and I doubt that anyone would have noticed them unless they were pointed out. He commented that, after doing the remedies, he was able to work in his office for longer periods of time than before and felt fresher at the end of the day. This was not surprising, because previously he had had poison arrows coming at him from all four corners. To correct such problems, you might place a potted plant in front of the shar, or perhaps install a mirror or hang a crystal (Figure 5A).

The placement of the desk is of extreme importance. You should sit facing the door. People who sit with their backs to the door feel uncomfortable and risk being "stabbed in the back" (Figure 5B). The desk should be as far from the entrance of the room as possible to give you a commanding view of your office as well as the door. If the shape of the room means that you cannot see the entrance clearly from where you sit, put up a mirror to give you a better view.

It is just as important for other people to see you as it is for you to see them. If you are tucked away in your office where no one can see you, you are likely to be overlooked for promotions, pay raises, or special projects. You need to be visible.

Although you should sit facing the door, you should not do so directly because this can intimidate visitors. Position

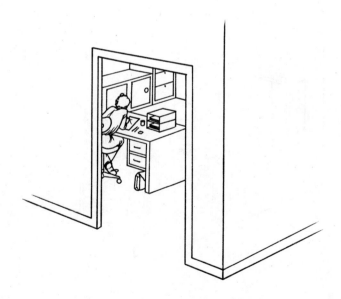

Figure 5B: Poor placement of desk

your desk at an angle to the entrance for best results (Figure 5C). Different angles produce different feelings, so you should experiment. Figure 5D shows three positive and three negative positions for the placement of desks.

In the past it was believed that the desk should be on either a north/south or east/west axis for best results. The ancients believed that you are more motivated to succeed when your desk faces north. You will feel more relaxed and at ease, however, when your desk faces south. If it faces east, you will be dynamic and inspirational. Facing west makes you more creative and full of good ideas.

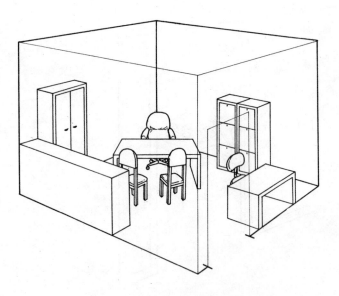

Figure 5C: Proper placement of desk

Figure 5D: Sample placements of desk

Keep in mind that your desk may look awkward and out of place if you adhere rigidly to these suggestions. It is important that your office look and feel comfortable. A desk placed in a strange position affects the appearance of the whole room and can also affect the flow of ch'i.

You can also use the five elements to attract the qualities that you are seeking. For instance, something black or blue on your desk will give you the effect of facing north even if it faces a completely different direction. This is because north relates to the water element.

In the same way, something red on your desk activates the fire element, which in turn will give you the effect of facing south. Something made of metal or painted white activates the metal element, and this gives you the advantages of facing west. Finally, fresh flowers, a potted plant, or something that is green will enhance the wood element and give you the feelings of facing east.

The Aspirations of the Pa-kua can also be useful in determining the most suitable position for you. The Wealth, Fame, and Career sectors are usually the most favorable positions for your desk to occupy.

The size of your desk, as well as the size of your office, indicates your power and status in the firm. You will progress faster in your career if your desk is larger than usual for your particular job.

Allow sufficient room behind your desk to get in and out of your chair easily. If you feel cramped, the ch'i will also, and you will be confined and restricted in what you are able to do.

Do not place your desk against a blank wall. This is a common practice for people who use computers, because it allows all the wires and cords to be hidden. In feng shui they should not be visible, but placing your desk against a blank wall is not a good way of concealing them. This position creates frustration and nervousness because of the inability to see what is going on behind you. If there is no alternative to this placement, hang a mirror on the wall so that you can see what is happening behind you. If this is not allowed, place a small mirror on your desk. If possible, hang up some bright, cheerful pictures on the wall and place a small crystal on your desk to attract the ch'i.

Do not sit with a window behind you, if at all possible. This placement indicates that you are lacking in support and may not be able to get help when you need it. Keep the blinds drawn if there is nowhere else to place your desk.

You can use the Aspirations of the Pa-kua on your desk as well. In the East, business people commonly place a metal container with a few coins in it in the Wealth location to activate prosperity. Place family photographs in the Family or Children sectors.

Make sure that the chair you sit on is comfortable and is adjusted to the right height. You will produce much more work from a comfortably aligned chair than you will from an uncomfortable chair of the wrong height. You will also feel happier and enjoy sitting behind your desk.

Avoid clutter in your office. If your desk always contains a mountain of files and papers, your life will be disorganized and frustrating. Do not store files in boxes on the floor. Keep your office as free of clutter as possible and your life will go much more smoothly.

The Four Houses

The Compass School of feng shui uses the eight trigrams of the I Ching to determine suitable directions for different activities. These eight trigrams can be divided into two groups: the East Four Houses and the West Four Houses.[1]

A simple formula is used to determine which group you belong to.

If you are male, subtract the last two digits of your year of birth from 100, and then divide by nine. We ignore the answer, but look at the remainder.

For instance, if you were born in 1956, we subtract 56 from 100, which gives us an answer of 44. We divide this by 9, which gives us a remainder of 8 (9 x 4 = 36, with 8 remaining). Another example, this time for a man born in 1946, looks like this: 100 − 46 = 54, and 54 divided by 9 is 6, with no remainder.

The formula is slightly different for women. If you are female, subtract four from the last two digits of your year of birth, and divide the answer by nine. Again, it is the remainder that is important.

Here is an example for a woman born in 1952. We subtract 4 from 52, which gives us 48. We then divide 48 by 9, and the answer is five, with a remainder of three.

One more example, for a woman born in 1975, looks like this: 75 − 4 = 71, and 71 divided by 9 is 7, with a remainder of 8.

For men and women, the remainder determines which grouping of houses you belong to.

If the remainder is 1, 3, or 4, or there is no remainder, you belong to the East Four Houses.

If the remainder is 2, 5, 6, 7, or 8, you belong to the West Four Houses.

For each grouping of houses there are four favorable and four unfavorable directions.

The favorable directions for members of the East Four Houses are north, east, southeast, and south.

The negative directions for members of the East Four Houses are northeast, southwest, west, and northwest.

The favorable directions for members of the West Four Houses are northeast, southwest, west, and northwest.

The negative directions for the members of the West Four Houses are north, east, southeast, and south.

By using a compass in your office, you will be able to determine the directions that are best for you. The ideal situation occurs when both the main entrance to the building and the doorway to your office are in directions that are favorable to you.

Many people in the East sit facing a favorable direction whenever possible. Consequently, their desks always face a favorable direction, and when they have important decisions to make they will ensure that they are facing a fortuitous direction. Gambling is extremely popular in Asia, and many gamblers will only do so when they are facing a fortunate direction.

General Offices

Special feng shui considerations are required with general offices where many people are working together in the same room.

Ideally, the room should be square or oblong in shape. Unusually shaped rooms create shars which can be hard to eliminate completely when there are several people working together in the same room.

The desks need to be arranged in such a way that there is plenty of space for the ch'i to flow in and around them. An arrangement like this also allows sufficient room for the people in the office to move freely. If possible, everyone in the office should have a view of the main entrance from his or her desk.

The worst position is to have your back to any door, as you risk being "stabbed in the back" (Figure 5E). For the same reason, it is also considered bad to have your back to an open area which people continually use to get from one place to another.

It is also not good to have desks too close to the main entrance. People sitting in these positions will be "clock watchers" and will leave for home as quickly as they can. They will not like the idea of overtime, either.

Desks that are directly facing walls create problems because there the ch'i cannot flow in front of them. Also, people working at such desks cannot see what is going on behind them. The remedy is to hang up a mirror to attract ch'i and to enable the person seated at the desk to see what is happening in the room.

Back door

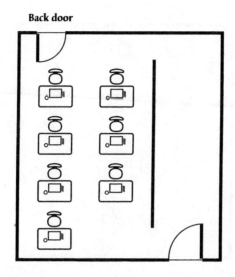

Figure 5L: Layout for a general office

Desks facing each other are not good from a feng shui point of view because this position is considered confrontational. A U-shaped arrangement of desks is almost as bad, because the people on the two long sides will be opposite each other. This arrangement is believed to generate friction and discord. An L-shaped arrangement of desks is believed to encourage some of the staff to gang up against other staff members. This creates a high absenteeism rate.

If there are only a small number of desks in the office, they can be placed at a diagonal to each other, simulating the shape of a pa-kua. It is important, however, to make sure that the angles of the desks do not create shars that

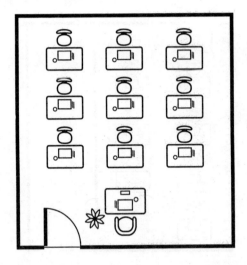

Figure 5F: Confrontational arrangement of desks

affect other desks. Room dividers, pillars, and overhead beams can also create shars that need to be remedied.

Any columns or pillars in the room need to be partially concealed with potted plants or mirrors.

The office manager should have his or her desk in the most favorable position in the room, which is usually in the corner farthest away from the entrance. This is the power position; anyone sitting here will progress in his or her career.

Sometimes I come across a general office where the office manager sits in a position facing the other staff, much as a teacher would face his or her pupils at school (Figure 5F).

This is the worst position of all from a morale point of view and is almost always confrontational.

Naturally, the main entrance needs to be protected from outside shars. The most usual shar associated with a general office is a long, straight corridor heading directly toward it. The remedy for this is to place several potted plants just inside the entrance. This not only remedies the shar, but looks attractive and gives the workers in the room a degree of privacy.

All electrical and telephone cables should be out of sight, if possible.

A bathroom directly off a general office is bad from a feng shui point of view, because the negative ch'i created in the bathroom will flow into the office, affecting everyone in it. Bathrooms were originally designed off a general office to encourage people to spend less time in the bathroom. It may serve its purpose in that regard, but it also encourages staff to find more harmonious places in which to work.

The lighting should be plentiful and evenly distributed. Extra lighting provided for any purpose should not cause glare to anyone else.

General offices should have a subtle color scheme. Bright and stimulating colors are likely to cause discord among the people working in the office. Color can also affect the moods of visitors to the office.

Cubicles

A cubicle is, in effect, a small office, usually consisting of three walls created by screens or dividers and an open side which acts as the entrance.

The cubicle needs to adhere to all of the requirements of an office. The occupant must not sit with his or her back facing the entrance, and the entrance itself usually needs some protection (Figure 5G). Even if there are no direct shars, hanging a crystal or wind chime over the entrance will increase the amount of ch'i coming in.

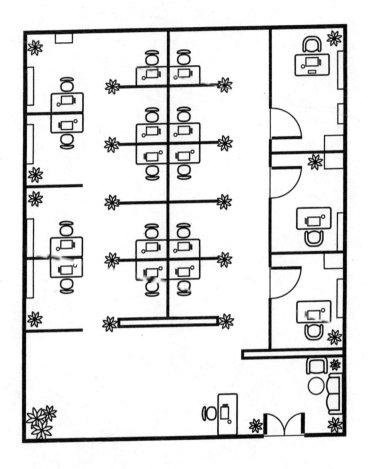

Figure 5G: General office with cubicles

6

The Home Office

In today's business world, more and more people are working from home, and this trend is likely to continue. My neighbors say that I'm "semi-retired" because I work from home and miss out on their daily commute to and from work.

There are definite advantages to working from home. My neighbors spend an average of forty-five minutes each morning and night commuting to and from work. This means that I gain an hour and a half of extra time each day. I can also take time off when required to attend to personal business or perhaps watch something one of my children is doing. I can work early in the morning or late at night. I can even work in my dressing gown, if I wish.

The disadvantages of working from home are that I am never entirely away from business. Because I work from home, people feel that they can call me at any hour of the day or night. It is rare for me to enjoy a meal without being interrupted by at least one phone call. Although I protect myself with an answering machine, I work in a highly competitive field and so I do not want to miss too many calls. I also find that I spend too much time working on the weekends as my office is too accessible. I can go into it to check something and suddenly realize that two hours have passed. If my office were situated several miles away from my home this would not occur.

My wife and I chose our current home because it was ideal for both a home and a business. Our front door provides a view of our recreation room and my waiting room. Clients can come in the front door and sit down in the waiting room without disturbing the family in any way. Friends and family come in the same door and go upstairs to our living area. When I have finished work for the day I go upstairs and figuratively leave my work behind.

If you work from home it is best to have a separate home office. This means that you are working while inside it, but once you leave it and, perhaps, close the door behind you, you are no longer at work. The best position for this room is to face south, which is the Fame direction. However, if it is to be used more as a study than an office, a better location is facing northeast, which is the Knowledge direction. Naturally, if customers visit you in your home office, it should be located reasonably close to the front door. (This, incidentally, is not a good place for a study, because you will be inclined to work rather than relax in it if it is close to the front door.) Years ago, when we lived in another house, my office was at the back. This meant that my clients had to walk right through the house to reach it. This was inconvenient for them and a discomforting intrusion for my family. It also did nothing for the image of my business.

Square and oblong offices are better than L-shaped ones. If your home office is L-shaped, place your desk in one of the areas and entertain your clients in the other. This symbolically turns the room into two separate rooms.

Once you have decided which room is to be the office, you can arrange it according to the Aspirations of the Pakua. My desk is in the Wealth position of my office. I have a separate writing room as well, and my computer is in the Fame sector of this room. The Wealth, Fame, Friends, Knowledge, and Career locations are all good areas for anything directly relating to your work.

Use the other areas as well, if appropriate. An acquaintance of mine designs and manufactures children's clothes. All of the designing is done in the Children area of her home office.

The placement of your desk is the most important part of the layout of your home office. The principles that were discussed in the last chapter apply in the home just as much as they do in an office building. Your desk should be placed in a commanding position, so that you are facing anyone who comes to the door of the room. This applies even if you have a mail order business and never get to meet any of your customers. People who sit with their backs to the door invariably get frustrated, and sometimes paranoid, even if they are the only occupant of the building.

The different items that you use in your business should be kept in auspicious locations. Your computer, telephone, and fax machine should be placed in areas that will benefit you. A friend of mine who is a hypnotherapist found that his business increased rapidly when he placed his telephone in the Wealth location. Another friend had her telephone in the Children sector of her home office.

"It was a wonderful way of keeping in touch with my children," she told me. "But I wasn't getting enough business calls." She stopped having those problems once she hung a crystal above the telephone to attract ch'i to it.

You need to encourage as much ch'i as possible into your home office. This enhances your concentration, creativity, and thinking. It also gives you more energy and increases the likelihood of success.

Good lighting is an excellent way to encourage ch'i and gives you a positive environment in which to work. Avoid glaring lights, though, as they create negative energy. Glare can also come in through the windows. Trying to shield your eyes from harsh light is extremely tiring, so you should avoid direct glare on your work. Use blinds or curtains to control this. It is better to have windows beside your desk, rather than behind you. You are said to be lacking in support when the windows are behind you.

The furniture and furnishings in your home office should be comfortable, but reflect a business use. For instance, it is better to use the type of chairs normally found in an office than to bring in a couple of chairs from the kitchen table. The furniture should be arranged for ease and comfort. Your office should appear spacious and not be cluttered with too much furniture. You will probably have bookcases in your home office. The individual shelves can cause shars; make sure that they do not affect the area where you spend most of your time.

Naturally, you should check your office for shars and eliminate or use remedies for these. Look outside the window to see if there are shars heading toward you from neighboring houses, power lines, roads, trees, or anything else. You will not want to spend too much time gazing out the window, but you should have a pleasant view all the same. It is considered bad feng shui to overlook a cemetery, church, police station, prison, hospital, or T-junction. You also do not want to look out at a hill directly in front of you. If the view is not pleasant, you may find it better to keep the blinds pulled for much of the day.

The color scheme of your office should reflect your personal element as well as the element that precedes yours in the Productive Cycle of Elements.

Fire burns and creates earth. If your element is **earth,** you should include some red in your color scheme

Earth creates metal. If your element is **metal,** include some yellow or brown in your color scheme.

Metal creates water. If your element is **water,** include some white or gold in your color scheme.

Water nurtures wood. If your element is **wood,** include some black or blue in your color scheme.

Wood burns to create fire. If your element is **fire,** use different shades of green in your color scheme.

You may also want to include colors that symbolize your aims. The colors used in Chinese restaurants are usually red and gold. This is not coincidence. Red means "good luck" and gold means "money."

It is important to avoid clutter in your home office. Clutter gradually constricts the amount of ch'i available and provides constant distractions. It also subconsciously gives you negative feelings of lack, loss, and limitation. You will feel your spirits rising as soon as you clear out the clutter. You will also become more focused, more creative, and have much more energy.

Many people who manage to avoid clutter elsewhere in their offices fail to realize that the mountain of paperwork on their desks also constitutes clutter. An astonishing amount of time can be wasted looking for lost items. At IBM, management established a policy of employees clearing their desks every night before heading home. This is done for security rather than feng shui reasons, but it makes good sense either way.[1] This may not seem so important if you are working on your own at home, but you will achieve much more when you work on a clear desk than you will when working on a tiny cleared space surrounded by clutter.

Many people do not have the luxury of a complete room to use as a home workplace. I wrote my first book on our kitchen table because there was no other space available. A friend of mine who writes comedy scripts uses part of his bedroom as his office.

When you are using part of a room as your workplace, you need to determine what the most important use of the room is. For instance, my friend the comedy writer is using the room to write in during the day and to sleep in at night. He began by using the room solely as a bedroom. Consequently, the bed was placed in the best position in the room. When he began using the room as his office, his desk was simply a card table in a corner. After a few months, he realized that he was unwittingly hampering his writing career. He bought an office desk and placed it in the most commanding position in the room. He moved the bed from one wall to another, and used a decorative screen to symbolically make the bed disappear during the day. By making these adjustments, he changed the emphasis of the bedroom from sleeping to writing. His career is thriving and he is now in a position to buy his own apartment. However, he is reluctant to do this because he feels that the energies around him in his office-bedroom are perfect.

7

Feng Shui for Success in Your Career

The whole purpose of feng shui is to help people lead lives rich in happiness, contentment, and abundance. If we can somehow channel those qualities into our working lives, we will be much happier and, consequently, much more successful in our careers. We can do this by making certain subtle adjustments at home and at work.

Usually, not much needs to be done. You might be tempted to hang wind chimes everywhere, and have crystals on every solid surface. It is better to make any changes slowly and gradually. Make a single change and then see what effect it has on your career before making another.

Remember, though, that feng shui does not do everything for you. Feng shui will help but it is not a magic wand. For instance, good feng shui makes it easier to get along well with other people at work because the beneficial ch'i makes your surroundings more harmonious. However, everyone is different and you will still have to make an effort to get along with disagreeable people. You will also have to be diligent and work to the best of your ability. Feng shui increases your luck, and helps make things go your way, but you cannot sit back and expect it to do everything for you.

At Home

We begin by looking at our home. Use the Aspirations of the Pa-kua to determine the Wealth and Career sectors of your home. Make sure that they both receive enough light and have no dark corners. Increase the amount of light, if necessary, to encourage more ch'i in.

Place something metallic in the Wealth location. Metal wind chimes are good here. Every time you hear them, you are reminded of the beneficial ch'i flowing through your home. You can also deliberately tap them every time you go past to encourage the ch'i. Make sure to get wind chimes with hollow rods because the ch'i moves up inside them. It cannot do that with solid rods. It is a good idea to get metal wind chimes that are painted either the color of your personal element or the color of the element that precedes yours in the Productive Cycle of Elements.

You may prefer to have an attractive metal ornament in the Wealth sector. It makes no difference how small or large it is, just as long as you notice it every time you are in this part of the house. This way it becomes a "silent affirmation." Every time you see it you are reminded of your purpose, which is to progress in your career.

When you leave home for work you should head in your Career direction, even if this requires that you drive away from your place of work. After heading in your Career direction for a minute or two, you can turn back and drive normally to work. Naturally, it is best if your work is in your Career direction, but you are helping your career by heading in that direction for a short while before continuing on to work.

Hanging a crystal in the Career sector of your home attracts ch'i and provides you with extra energy to help you in your work.

Your bedroom is also an important factor in career success. Your bed should be placed in the Wealth, Fame, or Career sectors of this room. Obviously, this is not possible in some rooms. If this is the case, align your bed so that your head is pointing toward one of those directions. This allows the ch'i energy to flow into you while you are sleeping. Whatever direction you choose, make sure that you can see anyone coming into the room without moving your head more than forty-five degrees.

There are three places where you should not put your bed. Do not sleep with either your head or your feet pointing toward the door. These are known as the "coffin" positions.[1] If the long side of your bed is against the same wall as the door, do not sleep with your back to the wall. In today's houses and apartments, many bedrooms have an en suite bathroom. Do not sleep facing the entrance to this room because you will breathe in negative ch'i all night long. All of these negative positions will hamper your career.

In addition, your bed should not be under an exposed beam. If there is no alternative, make sure that the beam runs down the bed, rather than across it. Hang two small bamboo flutes from the beam as a remedy.

Make sure that your bedroom receives sufficient light during the day. It is not a good idea to keep the curtains drawn during the day, because you want as much light and fresh air in this room as possible. This is particularly the case if you do any reading or studying in this room.

Activate the Career and Wealth areas of your bedroom. You can do this by increasing the light in these two areas, or by hanging up crystals suspended on red ribbon. You should also place an object made from your element in the Career sector. You may prefer to have something of the color that represents your element instead. For instance, a photograph in a red frame could represent the fire element, and a door painted blue could represent water.

Your dressing table should face the Career, Fame, or Wealth directions. This means that you will be facing a propitious direction while getting ready for work. However, make sure that the dressing table mirror does not face the foot of the bed, because this is bad from a feng shui point of view.

Your bathroom and toilet also need to be examined. They should not be in the north side of your house, because in this position they are believed to "flush away" your career. If there is more than one toilet in the house, use the one that is not on the north side. Keep the lid down and the door closed to a toilet on the north side of the house. It is also a good idea to place a large mirror on the outside of the door to symbolically make the room disappear.

If you have a home office or study, make sure that the desk is located in the Wealth, Fame, or Career sectors. Place a crystal or metallic object on the Wealth sector of the desk. You may prefer to keep any papers relating to your career here and use a large crystal as a paperweight.

At Work

To encourage success in your career, you need to examine your work space. You may have an entire office to yourself, or share space with several other people. You may have your work area somewhere inside a large factory. Whatever area you define as your work space, it needs to be assessed

Start by ensuring that your work space is protected from shars. Remember to look above you as well. It is important not to work directly under an exposed beam.

Look at all of the entrances to your building. If there is more than one, use the entrance that corresponds to your Wealth, Fame, or Career directions. This may not necessarily be the main door to the building. You subconsciously benefit by using the entrance door that best fits you. You can determine these directions by using the Aspirations of the Pa-kua over your office or work area. You will remember that the directions indicated extend indefinitely beyond the bounds of the room.

The eight directions are doubly important if you park your car in the basement of the building you work in. The entrance from the parking garage may not conform to your most favorable directions. It may be better to leave the parking garage and enter the building through another entrance.

Evaluate the main entrance to your work area carefully. It should be roughly the same size as the other doors inside the building. The door should open into the room, rather than against a wall. When it opens correctly, it should end up parallel to the wall it is on, rather than against the adjacent wall.

It is common to find doors with glass windows in them in the workplace. A solid door is better, because it gives you more privacy and ensures that you will be more productive. This may seem surprising to the executives in such offices, who like to be able to see what everyone else is doing. However, employees likes to be trusted, and a door containing a window sends a subconscious message that people are not to be trusted.

Place a pa-kua over your work area and make sure that your desk, or whatever other surface you work on, is placed in either the Career or Wealth sectors. You can do this using either the Eight Aspects or the Aspirations of the Pa-kua. The north and southeast are the best directions for career success. Face these directions while working, if possible. However, do not face these directions if it means putting your back to the door. It is more important to see people coming in than it is to face a positive direction.

Activate your work area with something to represent the metal element. You may place a small metal box containing a few coins in the Wealth location on your desk (the corner diagonally to the left from where you sit). This is a method that is commonly used in the East. Rather than a metallic object, you may use something that is white or gold in color to represent metal.

Metal is the perfect element to help you progress in your career. At its most basic, metal means money, and progress in your career means that you will reap steadily increasing rewards. It will not just happen on its own.

An acquaintance I met at a club I belong to works as a printer. He felt that because his printing machine was made of metal and was in the Wealth sector, he was doing all that was required to progress in his career. This was not the case. He had to add some item specifically intended to improve the feng shui. I persuaded him to hang a metal wind chime over the printing press and almost immediately he received a pay increase. He is now the foreman and is using feng shui all the time, at home as well as at work.

The size of the metal object is not usually of any importance. However, a friend of mine brought back a huge bronze elephant from a business trip to Taiwan. It was astonishingly ugly, and his wife refused to have it in the house. He took it to work and placed it in the Wealth sector of his office. He received two pay increases in quick succession and now his wife complains that he pays much more attention to the bronze elephant than he does to her.

Your desk, or work area, should be of sufficient size to reflect your status in the corporation. If you are a senior executive, your desk should be roughly five feet long and three feet wide. The most comfortable height is between twenty-nine and thirty-one inches. If you are a senior executive and your desk is much smaller than this, your status and power will be reduced and you will be less effective than you could be.

If you are a manager or mid-level executive, your desk should be approximately four feet long and thirty-three inches wide.

A secretary's desk can be any size at all. Usually, the longer this desk is, the better, because the secretary often has to handle several different tasks at the same time. The secretary's desk does not need to be as wide as the other desks. Anywhere between two to three feet wide is suffi- cient. The secretary's desk should be rectangular or curving in shape. An L-shaped desk sends a shar across the room.

Finally, walk around your work area. Try to see it with fresh eyes. Does it feel welcoming to you? You should enjoy coming into your work space because you spend such a large amount of your life there. If it does not feel comfort- able and stimulating, you will have to make further changes.

There is a certain pattern of movement known as the "Feng Shui Walk." This follows the sequence of numbers on the magic square that Wu found in the markings of the tortoise some five thousand years ago.

You start by mentally overlaying the magic square onto your office or work place. Stand in the number one posi- tion. This will be beside the wall on which the door to your office is located. Walk diagonally to the right ending up in position two. Keep on following the directions of the magic square, going from number to number until you finish on number nine. You will find this easier to do if you have this book open at Figure 7A. After you have practiced a few

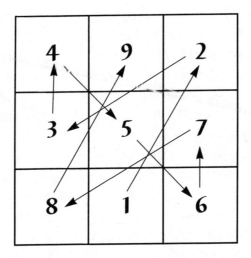

Figure 7A. The "feng shui walk"

times you will know the moves and will not need to refer to the diagram.

Naturally, you may not be able to walk in a straight line from one position to the next because of furniture and other objects that might be in your way. This does not matter. Simply move around them.

As you perform this exercise, try to see the room you are in as if you had never seen it before. You may notice that parts of the room seem more vital and vibrant than others. You may realize that an item of furniture looks out of place. The first time I did this in my own office, I realized that in one corner the wallpaper was marked and scuffed.

Although I spend hours every day in my office I had not noticed this before, but it must have been glaringly obvious to all of my visitors. Once the wallpaper was replaced, my office felt much more comfortable and I became more productive. If I had not done the feng shui walk it is likely that the wallpaper would still be marked and scuffed and unnoticed by me.

The purpose of the feng shui walk is to intuitively feel if everything in the room is in balance. Once you can do the walk in your work space and feel happy with every step, you will know that the ch'i is flowing freely and that the room is in harmony and balance.

How can your career not progress when you are working in such a pleasant environment?

8

Feng Shui Remedies

No matter how many feng shui problems your workplace contains, there is a remedy for every one of them. This is one of the wonderful things about feng shui. No property can ever be perfect. People have tried to build homes that were perfect from a feng shui point of view. However, as you know, the right direction for me may not be the right direction for you. Consequently, a house or other building erected purely for me and my needs might well be totally wrong for you—and this is purely from the placement of the front door, before we start to look at anything else.

Most of us are not in a position to build our own homes and workplaces. We need to buy an existing home, and either work for someone else on their premises or lease premises in which to conduct our businesses. This means that we have to accept situations that may not be ideal from a feng shui point of view.

Fortunately, now that you are familiar with feng shui, you will be able to look at your home and workplace with different eyes. You will see shars that you never noticed before. You will understand why certain rooms feel less comfortable than others. You will know why certain desk placements are better than others. You will be in control of the energies around you. You will be able to encourage the beneficial ch'i in to create harmony, contentment, and success in your career.

Exterior Remedies

Trees and shrubs are the remedies most often used to block shars aimed at your business premises. They can also be used to encourage ch'i. An attractive garden in front of your main entrance will encourage the ch'i to gather outside your front door, and much of it will then come inside. Evergreens are the perfect choice, because the branches of leafless deciduous trees can send shars towards you in the winter months.

The trees and shrubs should be well looked after, of course. Dead and dying plants create negative ch'i. Remove any sickly plant as quickly as possible and replace it with something healthy and vigorous.

Trees can be planted behind your business premises to provide protection and to symbolically serve as the hills at your back. Trees planted for this purpose must not be too close to the rear of the building. If they cast shade on the windows, they effectively prevent ch'i from entering, and this can affect the people working inside.

Trees can also provide protection from harsh winds and excessive noise. A row of trees not only looks attractive and provides protection, but also creates ch'i that benefits everyone. An acquaintance of mine has a large warehouse situated beside a cemetery. As you know, police stations, prisons, hospitals, churches, and graveyards are all considered shars in feng shui. He planted a row of trees to make this shar disappear and found that his business, which had stagnated for several years, began to grow again. His staff enjoyed spending their lunch hours sitting in the sun on the lawn between the warehouse and the trees. They returned to work invigorated and full of ch'i, which made them more productive, also.

You may have a large tree in front of your main entrance which acts as a shar. Rather than cutting it down, plant two more trees on either side of the main entrance, between the large tree and the front door. The three trees together form an arrow that points away from your front door. This effectively eliminates the poison arrow created by the single tree.

Beds of flowers look attractive and both create and attract beneficial ch'i. Flowers on either side of the path to your main entrance encourage the ch'i into your workplace and increase prosperity.

A pond or fountain can create good ch'i outside your work premises. If the pond has square corners, make sure that these do not create a shar directed at your building. Round or gently curving ponds are better than square or oblong ones. The water needs to be kept clean and, ideally, moving. Remember that fish, particularly goldfish, represent money in feng shui. A fish pond can bring many benefits to your business, but it needs to be looked after. Dirty, stagnant, or smelly water can create negative ch'i and produce an effect exactly opposite to the one you wanted.

A meandering stream in front of the main entrance creates ch'i and also brings financial opportunities your way. The same stream behind your building means the opposite. If you have such a stream behind the building, plant shrubs and bushes to make it as invisible as possible. A wall or fence would be even better.

Large decorative ornaments, such as a statue, can be used to stop the ch'i from leaving the property too quickly. A sculpture garden can also provide an area of stillness and tranquility where people can sit quietly for a while. It can be highly beneficial and restorative to meditate in an area like this before returning to the hustle and bustle of the workplace.

If the area outside your workplace is completely flat, it is said to be too yin. A large boulder or statue can be used to represent a hill, which symbolically provides yang energy to balance the ch'i. Pagodas were originally invented to serve this purpose.

Outside lights make wonderful remedies, particularly for unusually shaped plots of land. To remedy this, place a light at each of the front corners of the plot, and another one in the middle of the back boundary line.

If your workplace building is L-shaped, a light can be placed to symbolically make the building seem complete. This is a common remedy for houses as well.

If your plot slopes downhill, a light at the lowest point will effectively stop all the ch'i—and wealth—from rolling away from your premises.

Lights encourage the ch'i, even at night, and also provide additional security to your business premises.

Mirrors can be used to send back shars directed at your building. If the shar is directed at any of your entrances, place a small mirror directly above the affected door. In the East, a special pa-kua mirror is usually used. This is a small round mirror, centered in an eight-sided piece of wood, with the eight trigrams of the I Ching surrounding it. This creates a "yang" or aggressive mirror that actively sends the shar back. Mirrors are normally considered "yin," or passive.

Any size mirror can be used. In fact, mirrored glass walls act as huge defensive mirrors. However, you need to be careful with these, because they can create serious shars on neighboring buildings, and the occupants of these buildings may send the shars back to you.

Interior Remedies

Many people have told me that they are concerned about using feng shui remedies inside their workplace because they do not want to be considered eccentric. In certain circumstances this is probably a sensible precaution, but most of the time other people will respect what you decide to do. Fortunately, there are a large number of remedies that can be made without anyone realizing what you are doing.

I know a number of people who keep a crystal in the top drawers of their desks at work. This is because they are either not allowed to display them, or prefer not to. However, whenever their top drawer is open they receive some benefit.

One lady I know placed reflective tape on each of the drawers on her desk. It looks decorative and people often comment on how attractive it looks. Very few of them realize her real reasons for doing it.

Naturally, you do have to be careful with the remedies you use at work, because you have to live with the other people there every day. Fortunately, most remedies can be done discreetly and are simply invisible to everyone else.

A man who came to one of my classes many years ago keeps a large crystal in the Wealth position on his desk. Whenever anyone comments on it he simply tells them that it was given to him as a present. This is the truth but, as you know, it is only part of the truth. However, this partial explanation lets him keep it openly on display without other people realizing what he is doing.

A lady I know wanted to hang wind chimes in her office to encourage the ch'i in. She managed to do this by giving her manager a set of wind chimes as a birthday present and then suggesting that he hang them in his office. This enabled her to hang up a set of wind chimes in her own office without anyone taking notice.

There are eight interior remedies that can be used to eliminate feng shui problems. They are:

1. Light and light-reflecting objects

2. Living objects

3. Pleasant sounds

4. Moving objects

5. Heavy objects

6. Mechanical objects

7. Straight lines

8. Color

Light and Light-Reflecting Objects

Increasing the amount of light in your workplace is the most useful way to encourage more ch'i in. Anything that reflects light also can be used. Consequently, crystals and mirrors are extremely useful tools in feng shui. Naturally, a large mirror is better than a small one, and a chandelier is more effective than a solitary quartz crystal, but these are not always practical, particularly in the workplace.

You can activate any area of your workplace you wish by increasing the amount of light. If you feel that you are not receiving the degree of recognition in your corporation that you deserve, increase the amount of light in the Fame sector of your office. Obviously, you need to ensure that the additional light does not cause glare, particularly over your main working area.

Mirrors can be used in a number of ways. Their main purpose it to attract ch'i and to send shars back to where they came from. However, they can also make a small office appear bigger. They can correct an irregularly shaped room. They can also reflect attractive views from outside into your office or workplace. If you are unfortunate enough to work with your back to the door, a correctly placed mirror will allow you to see anyone who comes in without turning your head.

Mirrors can also make your business more profitable, because they symbolically double everything they reflect. A mirror by the cash register, for instance, symbolically doubles the money that is placed in it. Mirrors also, incidentally, double the number of customers you have.

Mirrors need to be placed carefully. If they are too small or hung too low, they can effectively "chop off" a person's head. Avoid mirror tiles. They create a grid effect which creates feelings of confinement and restriction.

Crystals and prisms attract the ch'i and allow it to spread out in every direction. They can be used to draw the ch'i away from an obvious shar, such as a staircase immediately facing the main entrance.

Crystal and glass vases serve the same purpose. Fresh flowers in a crystal vase act as a magnet to draw ch'i into your work space.

Living Objects

In the workplace, we are restricted in our choice of living objects. Plants are highly beneficial. They have been proven to lift people's spirits, and provide something for the occupant of the office to love and look after. People work more happily in an environment where live plants thrive. Potted plants can also be placed in front of shars to make them disappear.

Fresh flowers encourage beneficial ch'i. The bright colors and pleasant scents attract the beneficial ch'i, and anyone working nearby will feel a sense of well-being and positiveness. It is important that fresh flowers be replaced as soon as they start to wilt. Dead and dying flowers create negative ch'i, which has an adverse effect on the occupants of the room.

It is interesting to note that artificial flowers work just as well as live ones. A friend of mine makes beautiful origami flowers that she places around her office. Artificial flowers must be looked after and kept clean and fresh. Dusty, plastic flowers do not encourage ch'i. Dried flowers must not be used. After all, "feng shui" means "wind and water," and dried flowers have had all the water taken from them.

Fish are the only animals that are regularly found in the workplace. Aquariums are beneficial for a number of reasons. They allow people to have a view of water, no matter where they may be. Water and fish both mean "wealth" in Chinese symbology. Goldfish are the best fish to use because the color gold also represents wealth. Nine fish are the perfect number to have in an aquarium. The perfect combination of colors consists of eight goldfish, because "eight" means money in the near future, and one black fish for protection.

Fish are also believed to provide protection to your workplace. When a fish dies, it is an indication that a disaster has been averted, and the fish needs to be replaced right away.

Fish also relate to promotion, achievement, and success in exams. The ancient Chinese watched carp swimming upstream and leaping up waterfalls to reach their breeding grounds. This single-mindedness naturally reminded people of persistence, stamina, and ultimate success. In Imperial China, people had to pass examinations to progress in their careers as government servants and the fish became a motivational affirmation. If you feel you are ready for a promotion at work, place an aquarium in the Career sector of your office to activate the process.

Naturally, the aquarium needs to be well looked after. Any algae or foul smells coming from the aquarium create negative ch'i. An aerated aquarium is the best because the moving water actively creates ch'i in much the same way as a fountain does.

The best position for the aquarium is in the Wealth sector, though it can be placed anywhere. Aquariums also create silent affirmations. When people in the East see an aquarium, they instantly think of money.

People belonging to the fire element should be careful about using aquariums, because water puts out fire. If your element is fire and you want an aquarium, make sure that it is not overly large for the room for which it is intended. You may prefer to use ceramic or wooden fish to symbolize wealth and prosperity, rather than real ones.

Pleasant Sounds

I have a small bell at the entrance to my writing room and I make it ring every time I go in and out. It makes a cheerful sound and encourages the ch'i into my work room.

Wind chimes are just as effective as bells, and can be used indoors and out. Outdoors, they make pleasant music whenever the breeze catches them. In an office, you may have to gently tap them to hear the different sounds. This can be useful if you are working on something that requires all your concentration. Simply tap the wind chimes first to encourage the ch'i before starting on the project.

Wind chimes come in all shapes and sizes. Make sure that the one you choose contains hollow rods to allow the ch'i to rise in them. Use your personal element to help you select wind chimes. I belong to the fire element and have red wind chimes outside my main entrance.

Originally, wind chimes and bells were used to discourage ghosts and spirits who were believed to be scared of the sounds created. Ghosts can travel only in straight lines, so wind chimes can be used at the end of long passages, both to encourage the ch'i and also to discourage any mischievous spirits.

Moving Objects

Anything that moves can stimulate the ch'i. Flags, banners, ribbons, mobiles, and wind chimes all fit into this category. A fountain is an excellent example, because the moving water creates ch'i at the same time. Thanks to modern materials and technology, you can buy miniature fountains that can be placed almost anywhere.

Revolving doors and fans also fit into this category, because they help circulate the ch'i.

Heavy Objects

Heavy objects, such as statues or a large rock, can be used to effectively balance a room that seems to have most of the furniture on one side of it. They can also be used to slow down the ch'i in areas where it is moving too quickly. Overly large lobbies and long, wide corridors are both places where the ch'i gathers speed.

Heavy objects can also be used to stabilize difficult situations. Their solidity and weight counsel caution and patience, and reduce aggression.

Mechanical Objects

Anything electrical fits into this category. Computers are probably the most commonly found examples in the workplace, but fans, televisions, radios, and refrigerators are other examples. In the past, machinery of different types was used to encourage the ch'i. Today, a television set or stereo in the Family or Mentors area of the lunch room will activate ch'i and encourage friendships among members of the work force.

Naturally, all of these items can create negative, as well as positive, ch'i and need to be looked after. Electrical cables need to be kept out of sight as much as possible.

Straight Lines

Straight lines may sound like an unusual remedy, because straight lines also create shars. However, these straight lines are arranged to represent all or part of the eight-sided pa-kua and are consequently hung at an angle. Bamboo flutes, for instance, are commonly used as a remedy for overhead beams. Two of them are hung at forty-five degree angles to represent two of the eight sides of the pa-kua. They are traditionally hung on red ribbons with the mouthpieces facing downward. Flutes have always represented peace and contentment. Incidentally, two flutes hung above the cash register are believed to increase the profitability of the business, while at the same time repelling shoplifters and encouraging customers.

Furniture in a room can be arranged to replicate all or part of the pa-kua shape. This encourages open-mindedness and honesty.

Color

You are already familiar with the color of your personal element. Colors are used to stimulate the ch'i. Bright colors excite it, while softer colors quiet it. Red is a symbol of good luck. Black and blue represent the water element and, as you know, water means money. White and gold from the metal element also symbolize wealth.

In the West, we are used to quiet color schemes, but a small amount of a stronger color can be extremely effective in stimulating the ch'i of a room.

9

Conclusion

I hope you have found this book interesting. I also hope that it will prove helpful in your career. I know many people who were stagnating in their careers until they started using feng shui. Their progress has been a joy to witness. I hope that your career will prove just as successful once you start using feng shui in your workplace.

You probably became aware of many things that you would like to change at home and at work as you read this book. It is preferable to make any necessary changes one at a time. By doing it this way, you can evaluate the results of each change. Make one change and observe what happens for about three weeks. Then make one more change and wait again for a few weeks.

Some people become overwhelmed and think they have to change absolutely everything. I have not yet come across a situation where this is necessary. In fact, most people have to change just a handful of things to create perfect harmony in their workplace.

You will find it helpful to go through the workplace in a set order to ensure that everything is evaluated properly.

It surprises many people to learn that the process of enhancing your career actually starts inside your own home. Make sure that there are no shars affecting your front door. Your entrance area should be well lit to encourage the ch'i inside. Activate both the Wealth and Career sectors of your home using the Aspirations of the Pa-kua. You will probably want to activate other areas as well, but these are the two that need to be enhanced for career success. (My book *101 Feng Shui Tips for the Home* covers everything you need to know in order to improve the feng shui of your home environment.)

If you can, position your bed in the Wealth, Fame, or Career area of your bedroom. However, do not do this if the bed looks out-of-place in these locations. If you cannot place the bed in one of these three areas, you may be able to position it so that the head points toward one of these directions.

After enhancing your home, evaluate the building you work in. Start outside the premises, checking to see if the building itself gains support from either nearby hills or neighboring buildings. These represent the symbolic dragon and tiger discussed in Chapter One.

Look at the land surrounding the building to ensure that there is a balance of yin and yang in the environment. The building should fit comfortably with any neighboring buildings. If the building itself is small, for instance, but is surrounded by a forest of skyscrapers, the people working inside will feel constricted and uncomfortable.

After this, examine the front entrance carefully. This is the single most important aspect of workplace feng shui. Any shars that affect the front door have the potential to harm the business. They need to be remedied.

The door itself needs to be of a suitable size for the building. If it is too large, for example, your wealth can escape. If it is too small, the amount of ch'i coming in will be constricted, and this will have an effect on every aspect of the business.

Check that the front entrance faces one of your best directions (see Chapter Three). If you own the business, remember that water relates to money, and you are in business for a number of reasons, one of which is to make money. Consequently, it is considered better for the main entrance to face gently flowing water than to face one of your positive directions. A fountain or pond, especially a fish pond, in front of your building will bring financial benefits. However, these bodies of water need to be looked after, because dirty water creates negative ch'i which can harm the business.

Water flowing behind your premises means that financial opportunities are occurring that you cannot take advantage of. In this instance, it is better to erect a wall to hide the water from view. The wall symbolically causes the water to cease to exist, so that you will not be frustrated with opportunities that fail to pay off.

Stand at the front entrance and look inside the building. Ideally, you should see a pleasant, well-lit, welcoming lobby area. If the lobby is dark or gloomy, increase the amount of light to encourage more ch'i inside. If it is small, you may want to install a large mirror to symbolically double the size of the lobby.

Your building may have more than one entrance. If possible, you should use the entrance that corresponds to your Wealth, Fame, or Career directions whenever you enter or leave the building. Check that this door is not affected by shars, and that the entrance is well lit. Ensure that the area around it is kept clean and tidy to encourage the ch'i to use this entrance. (Approximately 80% of the ch'i comes in through the main entrance, and the rest comes in through other doors and windows.)

Once inside, the ch'i should flow smoothly around the premises. Check to ensure that the ch'i is not being affected by dark corners or clutter. Make sure that your wealth or good fortune are not being eroded away by dripping taps, or anything else that is not working properly. A door that sticks, a window that is hard to open, or anything else that causes frustration will create negative ch'i and affect your good fortune.

Carefully examine the effects that long straight hallways have on the rooms at each end. Any internal shars such as these need to be remedied. A mirror on the outside of the doors at each end of the hallway may be all that is required.

While you are doing this, you should check the doors on each side of the hallways. If they face doors on the opposite side of the hallway, both doors should be similar in size and positioned directly opposite each other. Doors that are slightly offset cause problems and arguments. The remedy is to hang a mirror next to each door.

Place a diagram of the Aspirations of the Pa-kua over a plan of the premises to ensure that each aspect of the business is being conducted in the right area. Do not hurry this part of the evaluation. What at first may appear to be the totally wrong placement may well be perfect when looked at carefully. For instance, you will probably want the CEO to have an office in the Wealth area. However, a different placement may work just as well, and you will need to look at the personality of this person to evaluate that. A CEO who is concerned with the well-being of the staff may prefer to have his or her office in the Family area. An older CEO who is gradually handing over power and authority may be happier in the Mentors area, where he or she can give advice and counsel.

Now look at the area where you, yourself, work. Start by looking for any shars that affect the main entrance to your working area. Then look for any internal shars. An acquaintance of mine suffered continual headaches until he moved his desk. He had been working directly under an overhead beam. The headaches disappeared completely when his chair was no longer under this shar.

Make sure that your own workspace is well lit to attract the ch'i. It should also appear cheerful and reflect something of your personality. Consequently, you should display photographs, ornaments, and other things that relate to you. It is a good idea to display something that relates to your own personal element. Recently, I was in the office of someone who was born in 1957. She has a small red porcelain rooster on her desk, which reflects both her element (fire) and Chinese zodiac sign (rooster).

Personalizing your work space in this way makes you feel more at home and relaxed. You will be happier and more productive in an environment that is pleasing to you.

If you have your own office, ensure that your desk is in a command position, where you can easily see anyone coming into the room. Use the Aspirations of the Pa-kua in the office and activate any area that you wish to enhance. In this situation it will probably be the Wealth, Fame, and Career areas. You do not necessarily need hanging wind chimes or oriental decorations. With thought, it is possible to enhance any area in a way that no one else would ever notice. The important thing is that you will know that the enhancements are there and that you are activating certain areas of your life to further your career.

You can do the same thing if your work space is part of a larger office. Use the Aspirations of the Pa-kua over the area that you consider to be your space, and activate the areas in which you wish to make progress. You can do this even if you work in a factory. You are likely to have your own personal space where you work. Check out and remedy any shars, and use the Aspirations of the Pa-kua to determine which areas to activate.

After a talk I gave some years ago, a factory cleaner came up to me and said that he did not have his own personal work space because he cleaned the entire building. He did have a small closet where he kept his cleaning materials, and wondered if this area should be activated. The closet was too small for him to enter; therefore, I told him that he needed to place the Aspirations of the Pa-kua over a plan of the entire premises and activate the areas he considered important. This, of course, created special problems, because the areas he wished to enhance were located in other people's work areas. However, after some thought, he placed some coins under the carpet in the CEOs office to activate his Wealth area, and a small crystal in the lining of a curtain in his Family area. To the best of my knowledge, these enhancements have not been noticed by anyone else.

Obviously, it is better if you can evaluate your premises with the support and cooperation of everyone working there. However, as you can see, it is possible to do whatever is necessary to enhance your own career without anyone else being aware of what you are doing.

Go through this book again, making notes of the things that need to be remedied in your home and place of work. You may come up with a list of ten or fifteen problems that need to be corrected. Write these down in order of importance. Remember, the changes you make at home are more important to your career than any changes you make in your workplace.

If you evaluate the list a second time, you are likely to find that the least important items on your list are effectively remedied by the changes you need to make to rectify the most important things.

Start working your way through the list. Become aware of the improvements in your life brought by each change you make. You will notice the quality of your working life steadily improve. You will feel happier, more contented, more fulfilled, and have a sense that you are on track with your career. As these changes occur, your motivation and job satisfaction will improve. Your superiors will notice these improvements in your life and you will be marked out for future promotion.

Use feng shui to harmonize your environment at every step of your career and you will find that it takes you exactly where you want to go. I wish you a bountiful harvest of ch'i and a highly successful career.

Appendix

Elements and Signs for the Years 1900 to 2000

Element	Sign	Year
Metal	Rat	Jan. 31, 1900 to Feb. 18, 1901
Metal	Ox	Feb. 19, 1901 to Feb. 7, 1902
Water	Tiger	Feb. 8, 1902 to Jan. 28, 1903
Water	Rabbit	Jan. 29, 1903 to Feb. 15, 1904
Wood	Dragon	Feb. 16, 1904 to Feb. 3, 1905
Wood	Snake	Feb. 4, 1905 to Jan. 24, 1906
Fire	Horse	Jan. 25, 1906 to Feb. 12, 1907
Fire	Sheep	Feb. 13, 1907 to Feb. 1, 1908
Earth	Monkey	Feb. 2, 1908 to Jan. 21, 1909
Earth	Rooster	Jan. 22, 1909 to Feb. 9, 1910
Metal	Dog	Feb. 10, 1910 to Jan. 29, 1911
Metal	Boar	Jan. 30, 1911 to Feb. 17, 1912
Water	Rat	Feb. 18, 1912 to Feb. 5, 1913
Water	Ox	Feb. 6, 1913 to Jan. 25, 1914
Wood	Tiger	Jan. 26, 1914 to Feb. 13, 1915

Wood	Rabbit	Feb. 14, 1915 to Feb. 2, 1916
Fire	Dragon	Feb. 3, 1916 to Jan. 22, 1917
Fire	Snake	Jan. 23, 1917 to Feb. 10, 1918
Earth	Horse	Feb. 11, 1918 to Jan. 31, 1919
Earth	Sheep	Feb. 1, 1919 to Feb. 19, 1920
Metal	Monkey	Feb. 20, 1920 to Feb. 7, 1921
Metal	Rooster	Feb. 8, 1921 to Jan. 27, 1922
Water	Dog	Jan. 28, 1922 to Feb. 15, 1923
Water	Boar	Feb. 16, 1923 to Feb. 4, 1924
Wood	Rat	Feb. 5, 1924 to Jan. 24, 1925
Wood	Ox	Jan. 25, 1925 to Feb. 12, 1926
Fire	Tiger	Feb. 13, 1926 to Feb. 1, 1927
Fire	Rabbit	Feb. 2, 1927 to Jan. 22, 1928
Earth	Dragon	Jan. 23, 1928 to Feb. 9, 1929
Earth	Snake	Feb. 10, 1929 to Jan. 29, 1930
Metal	Horse	Jan. 30, 1930 to Feb. 16, 1931
Metal	Sheep	Feb. 17, 1931 to Feb. 5, 1932
Water	Monkey	Feb. 6, 1932 to Jan. 25, 1933
Water	Rooster	Jan. 26, 1933 to Feb. 13, 1934
Wood	Dog	Feb. 14, 1934 to Feb. 3, 1935
Wood	Boar	Feb. 4, 1935 to Jan. 23, 1936
Fire	Rat	Jan. 24, 1936 to Feb. 10, 1937
Fire	Ox	Feb. 11, 1937 to Jan. 30, 1938
Earth	Tiger	Jan. 31, 1938 to Feb. 18, 1939
Earth	Rabbit	Feb. 19, 1939 to Feb. 7, 1940
Metal	Dragon	Feb. 8, 1940 to Jan. 26, 1941
Metal	Snake	Jan. 27, 1941 to Feb. 14, 1942
Water	Horse	Feb. 15, 1942 to Feb. 4, 1943
Water	Sheep	Feb. 5, 1943 to Jan. 24, 1944
Wood	Monkey	Jan. 25, 1944 to Feb. 12, 1945

Wood	Rooster	Feb. 13, 1945 to Feb. 1, 1946
Fire	Dog	Feb. 2, 1946 to Jan. 21, 1947
Fire	Boar	Jan. 22, 1947 to Feb. 9, 1948
Earth	Rat	Feb. 10, 1948 to Jan. 28, 1949
Earth	Ox	Jan. 29, 1949 to Feb. 16, 1950
Metal	Tiger	Feb. 17, 1950 to Feb. 5, 1951
Metal	Rabbit	Feb. 6, 1951 to Jan. 26, 1952
Water	Dragon	Jan. 27, 1952 to Feb. 13, 1953
Water	Snake	Feb. 14, 1953 to Feb. 2, 1954
Wood	Horse	Feb. 3, 1954 to Jan. 23, 1955
Wood	Sheep	Jan. 24, 1955 to Feb. 11, 1956
Fire	Monkey	Feb. 12, 1956 to Jan. 30, 1957
Fire	Rooster	Jan. 31, 1957 to Feb. 17, 1958
Earth	Dog	Feb. 18, 1958 to Feb. 7, 1959
Earth	Boar	Feb. 8, 1959 to Jan. 27, 1960
Metal	Rat	Jan. 28, 1960 to Feb. 14, 1961
Metal	Ox	Feb. 15, 1961 to Feb. 4, 1962
Water	Tiger	Feb. 5, 1962 to Jan. 24, 1963
Water	Rabbit	Jan. 25, 1963 to Feb. 12, 1964
Wood	Dragon	Feb. 13, 1964 to Feb. 1, 1965
Wood	Snake	Feb. 2, 1965 to Jan. 20, 1966
Fire	Horse	Jan. 21, 1966 to Feb. 8, 1967
Fire	Sheep	Feb. 9, 1967 to Jan. 29, 1968
Earth	Monkey	Jan. 30, 1968 to Feb. 16, 1969
Earth	Rooster	Feb. 17, 1969 to Feb. 5, 1970
Metal	Dog	Feb. 6, 1970 to Jan. 26, 1971
Metal	Boar	Jan. 27, 1971 to Jan. 15, 1972
Water	Rat	Jan. 16, 1972 to Feb. 2, 1973
Water	Ox	Feb. 3, 1973 to Jan. 22, 1974
Wood	Tiger	Jan. 23, 1974 to Feb. 10, 1975

Wood	Rabbit	Feb. 11, 1975 to Jan. 30, 1976
Fire	Dragon	Jan. 31, 1976 to Feb. 17, 1977
Fire	Snake	Feb. 18, 1977 to Feb. 6, 1978
Earth	Horse	Feb. 7, 1978 to Jan. 27, 1979
Earth	Sheep	Jan. 28, 1979 to Feb. 15, 1980
Metal	Monkey	Feb. 16, 1980 to Feb. 4, 1981
Metal	Rooster	Feb. 5, 1981 to Jan. 24, 1982
Water	Dog	Jan. 25, 1982 to Feb. 12, 1983
Water	Boar	Feb. 13, 1983 to Feb. 1, 1984
Wood	Rat	Feb. 2, 1984 to Feb. 19, 1985
Wood	Ox	Feb. 20, 1985 to Feb. 8, 1986
Fire	Tiger	Feb. 9, 1986 to Jan. 28, 1987
Fire	Rabbit	Jan. 29, 1987 to Feb. 16, 1988
Earth	Dragon	Feb. 17, 1988 to Feb. 5, 1989
Earth	Snake	Feb. 6, 1989 to Jan. 26, 1990
Metal	Horse	Jan. 27, 1990 to Feb. 14, 1991
Metal	Sheep	Feb. 15, 1991 to Feb. 3, 1992
Water	Monkey	Feb. 4, 1992 to Jan. 22, 1993
Water	Rooster	Jan. 23, 1993 to Feb. 9, 1994
Wood	Dog	Feb. 10, 1994 to Jan. 30, 1995
Wood	Boar	Jan. 31, 1995 to Feb. 18, 1996
Fire	Rat	Feb. 19, 1996 to Feb. 6, 1997
Fire	Ox	Feb. 7, 1997 to Jan. 27, 1998
Earth	Tiger	Jan. 28, 1998 to Feb. 15, 1999
Earth	Rabbit	Feb. 16, 1999 to Feb. 4, 2000
Metal	Dragon	Feb. 5, 2000

Notes

Introduction

1. Sarah Rossbach, *Interior Design with Feng Shui* (New York: Arkana Books, 1987), 113. Angel Thompson, *Feng Shui* (New York: St. Martin's Griffin, 1996), 147.

Chapter One

1. Ernest Eitel, *Feng Shui* (London: Trubner, 1873. Republished by Graham Brash, Singapore, 1984), 47.

Chapter Three

1. Richard Webster, *Feng Shui for Beginners* (St. Paul: Llewellyn Publications, 1997), xx.
2. Ibid., xxi.

Chapter Five

1. A much more detailed description of the East and West Four Houses can be found in *Feng Shui for Beginners* by Richard Webster, pp. 45–63.

Chapter Six

1. Wright Thurston, *500 Ways to Increase Your Income—IBM Business and Other Success Strategies* (6 audio cassette tapes) (Sandy: The Wright Thurston Company, 1987).

Chapter Seven

1. Richard Webster, *Feng Shui for Beginners,* 41. This placement of the bed is known as the "coffin" position because it reminds the Chinese of coffins lined up in the courtyards of temples waiting to be buried (according to tradition, people are not buried immediately after death; instead, the bodies are held until the "right" day for burial, as determined by Chinese astrology).

Glossary

Ch'i — The universal life force, or cosmic breath, that is found in all living things.

Compass School — The Compass School was developed approximately 2,500 years ago when the compass was invented. This enabled feng shui practitioners to use Chinese astrology, along with feng shui, to personalize it for individuals. It is more technical than the Form School, which was the original version of feng shui. Today, most practitioners use a combination of both systems when making their assessments.

Feng Shui — Feng shui literally means "wind and water." It is the art and practice of living in harmony with the earth. In feng shui, it is believed that if you live in harmony with the earth you will lead a life full of contentment, happiness, and success. Feng shui began in China approximately 5,000 years ago and until recently was little known outside the East. In the last twenty years, it has spread around the world and is now used virtually everywhere by architects, landscapers, designers, and business people.

Feng Shui Walk — The feng shui walk is a method of evaluating the feng shui of a room or building. The person performing the evaluation moves around the room, following the numbers on the magic square discovered by Emperor Wu. The person stands against the wall on which the main entrance of the room is located; his is position number one. He or she then moves to position two, three, and so on in sequence up to nine. As the person moves from one area to the next, he or she remains aware of everything that is going on and intuitively senses the areas where the feng shui is not correct. Once this has been determined, different remedies can be used to correct the imbalance.

Five Elements — In feng shui, we use the five elements of Chinese astrology: fire, earth, metal, water, and wood. Each element works in its own particular way and the different combinations of elements play an important part in feng shui.

Form School — The Form School is the original form of feng shui. In this school, a person looks at the geography of the landscape and evaluates it for the quantity and quality of ch'i available. The perfect site in the Form

School would be one in which your workplace is protected at the rear by hills and has a gentle stream meandering in front. Today, these positive attributes can be created artificially. The hills can be symbolized by nearby buildings or trees, and the water can be created by a fountain or pond.

Magic Square — A magic square consists of a series of numbers arranged in a grid in which all the horizontal, vertical, and diagonal numbers add up to the same total. The first magic square was the one found on the back of a tortoise by Wu of Hsia. That magic square was a three-by-three grid in which every row added up to fifteen.

Pa-kua — This is often known as the "great symbol" and consists of the yin/yang symbol surrounded by the eight trigrams of the I Ching.

Remedies — Remedies (sometimes known as "cures") are objects or actions that modify or eliminate the harmful effects of a shar. An example would be a mirror hung up to send a shar back to its place of origin.

Shan — This is a term used to describe the different shapes of hills and mountains.

Shars — Shars are often referred to as "poison arrows." They are straight lines containing negative energies (sometimes known as "shar ch'i") that bring the potential for bad luck and misfortune. They can be caused by any straight line or sharp angle that points directly toward you. A straight path leading from the road to your front door would be considered a shar.

Silent Affirmation — An affirmation is a short phrase or sentence that is repeated over and over again to instill positive thoughts into the mind. An example would be, "I create wealth and prosperity." In the East, people use silent affirmations, typically an object that creates a positive thought in the person's mind every time he or she happens to see it. For instance, a small metal container full of coins sitting on a corner of the desk will make the occupant think of money and success every time he or she notices it. An aquarium containing goldfish is a silent affirmation that makes the viewer think of success and advancement in his or her career.

Wu of Hsia — Emperor Wu of Hsia (sometimes referred to as Fu Hsi) lived approximately 4,800 years ago and is believed to have been the first ruler of China. No one knows if he ever actually existed, but he has been credited with many discoveries, one of which was the tortoise with the magic square on its shell. Wu is considered the father of feng shui, the I Ching, Chinese astrology, and Chinese numerology.

Yin and Yang — Yin and yang represent the two opposites in Taoist philosophy. It is believed that neither one can exist without the other. For instance, night is yin and day is yang. Without night, there could be no day. Yin and yang originally came from the two sides of a mountain. The shady, northern side was called yin, and the southern, sunny side was called yang.

Bibliography

Crawford, E. A. and Teresa Kennedy. *Chinese Elemental Astrology*. London: Judy Piatkus (Publishers) Ltd., 1992.

Eitel, Ernest J. *Feng Shui*. First published 1873. Numerous editions available, including Singapore: Graham Brash (Pte) Ltd., 1984.

Kingston, Karen. *Creating Sacred Space with Feng Shui*. London: Judy Piatkus (Publishers) Ltd., 1996 and New York: Broadway Books, 1997.

Lin, Jami. *Contemporary Earth Design: A Feng Shui Anthology*. Miami, FL: Earth Design Inc., 1997.

Lip, Evelyn. *Feng Shui for Business*. Torrance, CA: Heian International, Inc., 1990.

Rossbach, Sarah. *Interior Design with Feng Shui*. New York: Arkana Books, 1987.

Skinner, Stephen. *The Living Earth Manual of Feng-Shui*. London: Routledge and Kegan Paul, 1982.

Swan, James A., ed. *The Power of Place.* Wheaton, IL: Quest Books, 1991.

Thompson, Angel. *Feng Shui: How to Achieve the Most Harmonious Arrangement of Your Home and Office.* New York: St. Martin's Press, 1996.

Webster, Richard. *Feng Shui for Beginners.* St. Paul, MN: Llewellyn Publications, 1997.

Wong, Eva. *Feng-Shui: The Ancient Wisdom of Harmonious Living for Modern Times.* Boston, MA: Shambhala Publications, Inc., 1996.

Index

101 FENG SHUI TIPS FOR THE HOME

Richard Webster

For thousand of years, people in the Far East have used feng shui to improve their home and family lives and live in harmony with the earth. Certainly, people who practice feng-shui achieve a deep contentment that is denied most others. They usually do well romantically and financially. Architects around the world are beginning to incorporate the concepts of feng shui into their designs. Even people like Donald Trump freely admit to using feng shui.

Now you can make subtle and inexpensive changes to your home that can literally transform your life. If you're in the market for a house, learn what to look for in room design, single level vs. split level, staircases, front door location and more. If you want to improve upon your existing home, find out how its current design may be creating negative energy, and discover simple ways to remedy the situation without the cost of major renovations or remodeling.

Watch your success and spirits soar when you discover:

- How to evaluate the current feng shui energy in your home
- What to do about negative energy coming from neighbors
- How to use fountains or aquariums to attract money
- The best position for the front door
- How to arrange your living room furniture
- Colors to use and avoid for each member of the family

1-56718-809-5, 192 pp., 5 ¼ x 8, charts   **$9.95**